2000

REINTERPRETING THE AMERICAN DREAM

Persons and Ethics

Patrick Primeaux, S. M.

International Scholars Publications
Lanham • New York • Oxford

Copyright © 2000 by
International Scholars Publications
4720 Boston Way
Lanham, Maryland 20706

12 Hid's Copse Rd.
Cumnor Hill, Oxford OX2 9JJ

Library of Congress Cataloging-in-Publication Data

.

Primeaux, Patrick.
Reinterpreting the American Dream : Persons and ethics.
p.   cm.
Includes bibliographical references and index.
1.   Business ethics—United States. 2. Success in business—
United States. 3. Wealth—United States.   I. Title.
HF5387.P738   1999   174'.4—dc21   97-44061 CIP

ISBN 1-57309-252-5 (cloth: alk. ppr.)
ISBN 1-57309-251-7 (pbk: alk. ppr.)

∞™ The paper used in this publication meets the minimum
requirements of American National Standard for Information
Sciences—Permanence of Paper for Printed Library Materials,
ANSI Z39.48—1984

Dedicated to Michael Van
in his search for bliss

Contents

Foreword

There are many ways to read this book and there are many lessons to be learned from it. Although my good friend, Fr. Patrick Primeaux, S.M., has asked me to write a foreword, I almost wish he had asked me to write an epilogue instead. This is a book about what the American Dream has meant—both its strengths and its weaknesses—but also an extremely optimistic and ambitious book about what it might come to mean in the near future. My fear here is that I don't want to prejudice the reader into thinking my reading is the only correct reading of this book.

In fact, one of the great strengths of *Reinterpreting the American Dream: Persons and Ethics* is the author's ability to write on many levels simultaneously. Fr. Primeaux is at home in the popular culture, even as he offers his trenchant criticisms of it. It is clear that he is motivated not out of anger or fear as many moralists seem to be, but he writes because he loves who and what he is writing about. The author is equally at ease with the best of contemporary academic thinking. He refers to this literature judiciously and sparingly. He uses it to further his thesis, and never to flaunt it simply for its own sake. Further, and perhaps most importantly, he is a theologian who is willing to translate his particular vision of the world and God into an easily accessible vernacular.

In a word, Fr. Primeaux is an integrator. As such, he creates value by bringing together seemingly disparate elements and showing us how these parts interact with one another. He seamlessly weaves together insights gleaned from anthropology, business, (even) comics, literature, philosophy, politics, psychology, religion, and television. All the while, he never deviates from his thesis that humans are a complex combination of drives, needs, and forces.

In his words we are made up of bodies, minds, hearts, and souls. We are physical beings, but not only physical beings. We are rational, but not solely rational. We are emotional, but more than emotional. We are spiritual, but not exclusively so. Any view which does not factor all of these elements into the human equation is lacking. The goal is a view of life which is searching for the elusive point of equilibrium.

In the end, he demonstrates to us nothing less than the possibility that we can be better humans by giving us a better theory of what it means to be human. By paying closer and better attention to our experiences and dreams we become more aware of our vast human potential. By taking our own identities and values seriously we begin taking small steps toward self-improvement and enhanced consciousness. By being open to alternative interpretations and considering newly emerging theories of organization, we recognize the infinite possibilities inherent in human evolution.

In the very last chapter of this book Fr. Primeaux describes those rare individuals who move beyond the "disconnections of independence and the connections of dependence into the interconnections of interdependence." He writes carefully and with precision. But most importantly, he writes convincingly:

They raise the bar, push the envelope to the edge, focusing on interrelationships and the possibilities of moving beyond relationships with ourselves, or others, or nature, or God in particular. They want to know how it all comes together, and adopt a perspective for their own lives, and life in general, which concentrates on all of them for a consistent and simultaneous appreciation of the whole. They tend towards abstraction and idealism, but, at the same time, towards translating that abstraction and idealism into implications for the everyday world of division and separation, tension and conflict.

This paragraph is worthy of contemplation. It climaxes a vision worthy of emulation.

In the remainder of this brief foreword, I would like to highlight specifically what it is that I learned from reading and re-reading this book. Among other things,

Fr. Primeaux provides an excellent example of how to write authentically about ethics in a way that takes the religious outlook seriously, but also recognizes the realities and benefits which have been brought about by an increasingly pluralistic world. In other words, he provides a method for doing serious and creative work in religious ethics, even in a post-modern age.

Throughout this text, Fr. Primeaux holds fast to a number of working principles. Although he does not explicitly articulate these themes, they provide both constraints and inspiration. Let me try to identify some of these. I do this because I believe that in following him, all of us will learn better how to integrate our lives and discover deeper and deeper levels of meaning. His message will obviously resonate in his own Catholic community, but what is more important to me, is that it will also impact larger and larger communities, as well.

Fr. Primeaux's first principle is obviously *honesty*. I'm not only talking here about an unbiased disclosure of the facts, but I'm talking about what might be described as a "passion for truth." What strikes me most about his writing is the fact that I never doubt that he believes what it is he's writing about. Like all great writers, he writes first to satisfy himself. The ideas contained in this book, are not merely intellectual ruminations, but they give us a glimpse into Fr. Primeaux's own value system. While I don't always agree with his conclusions (in fact, in many instances we have strong differences of opinion), I nevertheless always take them seriously because I know that he does.

Fr. Primeaux recognizes that honesty alone, no matter how passionate, is insufficient. The second implicit principle which I derive from his work is *respect* for others. Perhaps he believes that everyone else is as honest as he is. But, whatever motivates him, his writing reflects his deep belief that no one individual, no one approach, be it a religion or an ideology, has a monopoly on truth. His type of respect goes beyond mere toleration. In Fr. Primeaux's world, the goal is to look actively for the truth everywhere.

In this respect, he reminds me of the great Jewish theologian, Rabbi Abraham Isaac Kook, the first chief Rabbi of Palestine, a post he held for sixteen years before his death in 1935. Rabbi Kook, born in 1865 in Grieve, Latvia, was a rare individual who combined a world-class intellect with practical savvy. His was not a world where everyone is selfishly pursuing his or her own interests, but rather a world where our common interests and our common humanity are thought to be what makes us most human.

Rabbi Kook, like Fr. Primeaux, was convinced that the solution to so many of our contemporary problems, would be found only when everyone, including leaders, would recognize the need for searching out truth beyond our normal and familiar boundaries. Rabbi Kook gives expression to this idea in almost poetic terms:

A chaotic world stands before us as long as we have not attained to that degree of higher perfection of uniting all life-forces and all their diverse tendencies. As long as each one exalts himself, claiming, I am sovereign, I and none other, there cannot be peace in our midst...All our endeavors must be directed toward disclosing the light of general harmony, which derives not from suppressing any power, any thought, any tendency, but by bringing each of them within the vast ocean of light infinite, where all things find their unity, where all is ennobled, all is exalted, all is hallowed (as quoted in *Abraham Isaac Kook*, translation and introduction by Ben Z. Bosker: The Paulist Press, 1978, 8).

Rabbi Kook was no secularist and neither is Fr. Primeaux. Nevertheless they both recognize a truth inherent in the secularists' approach, a truth missing from a purely religious perspective.

In order for a religiously-based ethics to be successful in the contemporary world, to affect behavior in a positive way, it needs to be *pragmatic*. This is a third implicit principle of his. While it comes perilously close to being a tautology, it is so often forgotten by religious men and women that it is worth emphasizing here. This principle goes beyond the respect discussed above and obviously suggests a non-dogmatic approach to religious ethics. A pragmatism true to religious roots requires the inclusionary attitude of both/and as opposed to the either/or mentality so often associated with a religious mind set. It is a theme which permeates this book. What Fr. Primeaux is trying to teach us is that if we are smart enough and wise enough it just might be the case that we can have our cake and eat it too.

His fourth principle is the principle of *growth*. Wherever we find ourselves today, there is always room for improvement. Human nature is not fixed once and for all, but humans have the potential for growth. Our own nature is something that we ourselves have a say in. As he puts it, "We are proposing a fundamental change, a transformation or conversion, from the ways in which we have learned to identify ourselves and ours ethics to new and different ways of appreciating ourselves, our motives--and to the translation of those motives into action and reaction."

Finally, Fr. Primeaux has recognized that a religious ethics must put *meaning* and the human search for meaning at its center. In the end, he recognizes that meaning is not something that will be imposed upon us from above, but at least in part, we "create meaning for ourselves as persons, and for our organizations as corporate persons." In a sense, meaning is a human choice. He continues: "Meaning is attributed to a convergence of concern for oneself, for others and nature, and for that 'something other' than either of these. Meaning is not, then, a matter of emphasizing one or the other, but a synthesis of all three for a new appreciation of what it means o be a person living and working in America."

I might quibble that this vision is appropriate not only for Americans, but also for all citizens of the newly emerging global world. But everyone interested in continuing Fr. Primeaux's discussion must recognize that it should begin exactly where he leaves off. In other words, a religious ethics appropriate for the post-modern world must recognize with no apologies that the search for meaning and significance is the central human activity.

In 1965, Stamford University Press published an essay by Rabbi Abraham Joshua

Heschel which he had delivered two years earlier as the Raymond Fred West Memorial Lecture. The name of the book is *Who is Man?* It is a brilliant and concise book written by one of the greatest twentieth century Jewish religious leaders. It is the work of a genius in the prime of his writing career. I don't believe it was ever his intention to really answer the question in his title. I don't believe he thought there was one answer for all times. I do believe, however, that it was his hope that people from all walks of life would continue asking this question as if everything else we care about hinged upon it.

From the perspective which my tiny spot on the universe offers, the best thing I can say about *Reinterpreting the American Dream: Persons and Ethics* is that Fr. Primeaux continues to ask the right question. In recognizing humans as precious, unique, and sacred, he does so in a mature and fair way. Rabbi Heschel wrote that "accepting the sacred means not only giving up claims, but also facing a unique dimension of reality...To sense the sacred is to sense what is dear to God. Its mode of being differs from the modes of being of other qualities." Fr. Primeaux's vision agrees with this and even helps us understand it in more precise and contemporary terms.

Moses Pava, Ph.D.
Alvin J. Einbender Chair of Business Ethics
Yeshiva University, New York
January 1, 2000

1. Experiencing

Influenced by People and Organizations
First, Towards Selfishness and Greed
Then, Towards Empathy and Sacrifice
Perhaps, Towards Yearning and Aspiring

Experience, the dictionary tells us, is "the actual observation of facts or events, considered as a source of knowledge" and "the events that have taken place within the knowledge of an individual, a community, mankind at large, either during a particular period or generally." It also refers to "what one has undergone" and "the fact of being consciously affected by an event."[1] Based on this definition, we know ourselves from what we have observed, from what we have undergone, from how we've been affected by facts and events.

There is an underlying implication of passivity and receptivity in these words and phrases. Something has happened; something has been done; something has been said. That something has entered into us. What is that something? It is

---

[1] Edmund S. Weiner and John Simpson, eds., *Oxford English Dictionary* (Second Edition) On Compact Disc (Oxford: Oxford University Press, 1998).

everything that has entered into us through our senses; anything we have seen, heard, touched, smelled, tasted.

There is also an underlying implication of profusion and confusion. Whirling around within us at every given moment are thousands of conceptions, perceptions, and impressions received from the outside. Some dazzle and excite, inspire and enliven; others settle and subdue, depress and discourage. Some direct us outwards, towards other people, towards nature, even further towards the cosmos, even to the divine; others direct us inwards, towards ourselves. Some change us; others confirm us. Some lead us towards order and organization; others towards disorder and discord. All would have us accept and acquiesce, rendering us passive receptors not only of perceptions and impressions, but of underlying schemes and strategies, plots and programs.

To describe these implications, the theologian Richard Niebuhr uses the image of a person listening to the radio. "Since the radio is an extension of the ear, the radio listener occupies the position of a target into which impulses of energy penetrate from the whole globe and its environment." The radio listener is receptive to "quanta or radiations" which communicate "waves of energy: sentences and expressions, harmonies, images, color arrangements, and so forth" which influence us coercively and persuasively.[2]

The third implication is the loud and clear message that what we are experiencing is the power of others over us. "But what is clear," he claims, "is that the radio listener lives in a radial world of energy, and the device itself is but one of the instruments that are transforming him [and her] into, and reminding him that he is a being for whom immediate reality is power, power driving and moving him,

---

[2] Richard R. Niebuhr, *Experiential Religion* (New York: Harper & Row, 1972), xiii.

distracting and destroying him, healing and shaping him. He is a radial man in a radial world."[3] Reality is power.

As radial men and women, we cannot ignore or dismiss the many influences constantly bombarding, pulling and pushing in one direction or another, towards one objective or another. Passive and determined, what can we do? Given the pervasive, overwhelming power of these determining influences forming and shaping us, the person has no choice but to follow, to obey.

We have been formed and shaped to meet the expectations of others. We have been programmed by a huge conspiracy of interconnecting people and institutions motivating us to meet their objectives; prompting us to pursue their patterns of thinking, speaking, and acting. From the time we're born to the time we die, we're told what's important and not important, what to eat and not to eat, what to wear and not to wear, where to go and not to go, what to buy and not to buy, what to think and not to think, what to do and not to do. And we do as we're told.

We cannot escape those influences, or the ways we have been coerced and persuaded to assume rational, emotional, and spiritual identities as persons. Not as obvious is the impact of those same influences on our ethics, on the ways we determine good and evil. Neither as apparent is the degree to which the people and institutions of our experience would expect us to identify ourselves as passive and dependent.

These many influences determine the perspectives from which we engage ourselves with the world around us, and also the values represented by each of these perspectives. Some are obvious, so apparent that they cannot be missed. Others are

---

[3]Richard R. Niebuhr, xiii. "Of course, many other instruments illustrate this taut and fatiguing watchfulness: the radio telescope, radar, U-2 aircraft, satellites, and so forth. But the familiar word radio symbolizes the situation of the watcher better than any other word or image can. For radio, as dictionaries tell us, derives from radius, meaning ray, and, by association, wave and packet: of light, of sound, of electricity, of atomic energy."

more subtle and unrecognized. All of them would have us be independent, dependent, and interdependent. All of them would have us focus in on ourselves, on others and nature, and on that "something other" than ourselves, people, and nature which we often identify as God. Accompanying each of these perspectives is a set of values which, once activated and exercised, become more representative of our identities than anything we think or say. Whichever of these perspectives we assume in response to the power of these determining influences identifies us and our actions.

Influenced by People and Organizations

We obey. We follow. We adhere to the expectations of people and organizations. Parents tell us to make something of ourselves and we do. Friends tell us where to go, and we go. Government tells us to pay taxes, and we do. Religion tells us to pray, and we do. Education tells us to study, and we do. Business tells us to make money, and we do. What they are all telling us is to obey, to comply, to submit, to invest in their objectives and their values. They control us and determine us in ways all-too-apparent and in ways all-too-subtle.

Often, when we relate our experiences, we do so with respect to new or significant insights or events. As formative as these may be, we also need to acknowledge that among our experiences are the common, ordinary occurrences of every-day life, especially patterns of verbal and nonverbal communication, and of obvious and subtle behavior. These commonplace experiences are actually more determinative of our identities and our ethics than the unusual or extraordinary experiences we discuss among friends and acquaintances.

4

Shaped by People. Whether from nature or nurture, everything about us is given or inherited, determined for us or imposed on us. Do we choose our parents, or the color of our skin, or the color of our hair? Do we choose the neighborhoods, the cities, the states, or the nations where we grow up? Do we choose our grandparents, our aunts, uncles, and cousins? Do we choose the churches, temples, or mosques we attend? Do we choose our friends, whom to like and whom to dislike?

Clearly, our bodies are inherited from our fathers and mothers. We recognize that everything about the body, from the color of eyes to disposition to heart failure, is given to us. In school we learn more about the body, its organic connections, its complex and intricate performance. We also absorb, often unconsciously and informally, the scientific laws governing its functions, both internally and externally. We need to breathe; we need to be fed; we need to be clothed. That knowledge, too, is given.

Do we need to be clothed in the latest styles? Even our tastes and preferences in clothes originate in others. They are given to us by fashion designers, encouraged by advertisers, influenced by the example of family and friends, and also by institutional expectations. We dress to meet individual and corporate expectations. We wear dark colors to funerals, and brides wear white for weddings. We wear suits to work during the summer and the winter; tee shirts and shorts to school during the summer, and jeans and sweaters during the winter. Why?

We dress according to the weather, warmly when it's cooler, sparingly when it's hotter. The weather, too, determines and exercises power over us. It, too, is given. So, too, are all of nature, and its rivers and valleys, trees and grass, oceans and mountains, beaches and ski slopes; its hurricanes and earthquakes. So is the immediate climate of our homes and neighborhoods. In the major airports of the Northeast people move more quickly to ticket counters and gates than they do in the major airports of the South. Colder climates elicit a faster, more energetic, more invigorating pace. Conventional Wisdom claims that the heat and humidity of the South result in slower patterns of speech as well as action.

To a great extent, the locations of those homes and neighborhoods reflect a whole range of determinants we take for granted. Where we grow up is a function not only of our parents' aesthetic preferences, but also of their practical preferences for proximity to or distance from work, schools, families, and friends. It is also an indicator of socioeconomic status, and of the values accompanying that status. From an early age, we're immersed in a sea of expectations, often too subtle to conceptualize or verbalize, but nevertheless impressed upon us decisively and definitively.

From birth, through childhood and adolescence, even into adulthood, we are overpowered and overwhelmed with attitudes and dispositions which, consciously or unconsciously, we take into ourselves. Our attitudes towards others are shaped by the ethnic jokes we hear and repeat for our own amusement and the amusement of others. Our own facial expressions, hand gestures, body language in general imitate those of our parents, friends, and acquaintances.

We are formed, shaped, and molded by the people around us, especially people who have determinative power over us. In other words, we have been influenced to meet the demands and expectations of others. Our past histories, our past experiences have taught us to value obedience more than any other virtue, or value, or ethical imperative.

The control of the many influences that determine our lives elicits passive compliance and obedience. That compliance and obedience are also directed towards the individual, and to individual self-interest, for the individual who obeys is rewarded. It is in our best interest to obey. People and institutions converge to make demands on us as individuals, and to pat us approvingly on the shoulder for obeying.

Formed by Institutions. Among these institutions are the families in which we grow up, the schools in which we are educated, the churches in which we pray, and the businesses in which we work. Nor can we exclude the media, and its influence on us. More often than not, we focus our attention on their immediate impact on our lives, what they ask of us here and now. Because of that focus, we fail to realize the more indirect ways they influence us, our values, our ethics. We also fail to realize the more subtle ways they define us as persons and our actions as ethical agents.

Perhaps more subtle is the manner in which these institutions are structured, and the ways in which the organizational structure elicits its own expectations. Attentive to organizational structure, we begin to see just how much the organizational structure corresponds to an identification of the person as primarily individualized and isolated from others. Closed doors of corporate offices allow the individual space to accomplish individual tasks. That individual is so often identified with the task, that personal identity is equated with it. We first ask, "What do you do?" to identify people.

To a great extent, the organizations of our social institutions are structured for control, for obedience and compliance. They are also structured for individual self-interest, and for promotion to higher positions of power on the basis of obedience, as a reward for obedience. Other words come to mind— loyalty, efficiency, character, intelligence, creativity— but the bottom line is whether or not these other attributes will be directed towards meeting the direct or indirect expectations of the institutions in which we grow, become educated, establish careers.

Governments demand that we pay taxes and follow the law. They, too, assume personal identity as a matter of individual distinction, with rights and duties ascribed to the individual, and, in doing so, encourage values and ethics supportive of individual self-interest. The "one-man one-vote" doctrine images that perspective. We vote for men and women who will promote our interests. The relational, communal dimension of "the common good" is reduced to secondary status, based on the prior assumption that what is good, right, and just for individuals is advantageous and appropriate for the majority of individuals, if not for all individuals.

In our schools, for example, we find the same assumptions and the same emphases on the isolated individual and on self-interest we find in government. The classroom is structured for individual learning. On the most basic level, we sit among others to learn what we can for ourselves as individuals. We study as individuals; we're examined as individuals; we're graded as individuals. Accordingly, the values they promote and encourage are, implicitly and inherently, those of individual self-interest.

The teacher leads, the students follow; the teacher commands, the students obey. The more persuasive and convincing the teacher's leadership, the more likely students will meet the expectations of the course, perhaps even moving beyond them. The more coercive and forceful the teacher, the more aware of, and sensitive to expectations students will be. Consistent with these demands and expectations is a system of rewards and punishments which distinguishes and separates students from one another. The traditional grading system ranks students individually, distinguishing them from one another on the basis of intelligence and diligence, and separates them into distinct castes of good, mediocre, and poor. It also influences personal identity, and suggests that personal identity can be rationally and numerically determined, especially in comparison and contrast to other students.

Even more influential and determinative, however, is the often subtle and unconscious connection between compliance and reward. The student who obeys most is rewarded most, and parents and friends are all too anxious to express their approval for those who excel. The classroom's organizational structure is influential and determinative, especially in its subtle, even unconscious, emphasis on obedience and compliance as significant determinants of personal identity and personal valuation.

That identity and valuation are, however, based on an appreciation of the person as primarily individual, isolated, and competing for distinction. That isolation is determined primarily in rational, numerical, and quantifiable terms. It's not a matter of a person becoming a number so much as personal identity being determined by numbers, and by one's status along a mathematical continuum stretching from least to most, lowest to highest. The manner in which one is measured, one's place along that continuum, identifies the person in terms of distinction from others. Numerically calculated separation and distinction, qualification and quantification suggest contrast and opposition. These personal and organizational influences would want us to focus personal identity on individual isolation and distinction, and to maintain and enhance that isolation with obedience.

Moreover, we find that concentration on isolated individuality accompanied by a concentration on obedience to authority. From experience, especially the experience of social institutions, we find ourselves to be passive recipients of assumptions and presuppositions, of corresponding organizational structures and ethical expectations consistent with both. The structure of institutions, the ways in which they order and organize people elicit their own behavioral expectations. They, too, determine, what we are to say, how we are to dress, how we are to act, what is right and what is wrong.

Yet, we know that we are not determined simply towards individual self-interest. We are also the willing recipients of influences which direct us towards others, towards relational cooperation. These influences are, however, relegated to secondary status. The majority of our relationships, and the majority of the time we spend with others, is consumed by the overpowering influences promoting individual self-interest. Also overpowering are the influences which correspond to an appreciation of personal identity with respect to obedience.

What do we do about these determinative influences, especially those arising from social institutions? We seem to have no control over them. We have no apparent means of stopping them from entering into us, from directing us towards meeting their expectations. They come from everywhere, impinge on us, invade our senses, and we are powerless to impede or evade them.

We obey. We acquiesce to their power because it is in our own individual self-interest to do so. We obey because we will be rewarded rather than punished, and the reward for obedience is advancement and promotion to positions of power and control. From the many determining influences that exercise power and control over us— both individual persons and corporate institutions— we learn to be obedient so that one day we can be in control.

We also attend to the media, especially to its compelling, seductive advertisements, setting standards of dress and decorum, conduct and behavior, housing and transportation, to which to aspire. They also tell us what we need to reflect our acquiescence to their determinative influence. What we hear on the radio and see on television, whether in commercials, news reports, or programming we want for ourselves.

So, we're told, "Make something of yourself." Because of a series of earlier influences, not the least of which is what everyone around us is doing, we know exactly what that means: study hard, get a degree, get a high-paying job, work hard, marry early, buy a home in an upwardly-mobile neighborhood, get a promotion, make more money, buy a better home, and on and on, and on, and on. It's the recipe for success, and, of course, success will lead to happiness.

We're also told, "We really don't care what you do; just as long as you're happy." And, we know exactly what that means as well: achieve the in control that comes with wealth. Pursue an ethics which concentrates on achieving that control. The subtle, underlying message is that independence for ourselves, and control over our own lives, and the lives of others, is not only possible, but desirable.

First, Towards Selfishness and Greed

What can we conclude from these observations? First, we realize that, among all its meanings and nuances, experience refers to power. Second, we see that power is manifested though obedience and control. What experience teaches us is that we are first obedient that we might someday have control, and that we attach value primarily to control. Why do we obey, conform, and acquiesce to the control of others? We do so to someday assume that control for ourselves, and to move from being obedient to being in control.

What we have been seeing and hearing all of our lives is the American Dream in theory and practice. What we experience is a directive to get out there, land a job, work hard, make money to feed, clothe, and provide a living for ourselves and our families. We are to achieve, to apply ourselves, to make something of ourselves. We are to make money, as much as we can, more than our parents.[4] We are to strive for wealth and distinction.

---

[4] Peter Peterson, "What my Father Knew About Economics," *Facing Up: How to Rescue the Economy from Crushing Debt and Restore the American Dream* (New York: Simon & Schuster, 1993), 48-68.

What we absorbed from the many people and institutions influencing us are the basic values of the American Dream: wealth and distinction. We also learned that we have to do it for ourselves. We have to concentrate on ourselves, distinguish ourselves from others, and make it or break it on our own. We are to be autonomous individuals providing for ourselves, becoming self-supporting and self-sustaining. We are to break away from the pack, differentiate ourselves from others, and do so through achievement, wealth, and status. We are to be strong, powerful, and independent in our own right and through our own devices.

All around us, we're seeing men and women achieving, making money, and reaching for status. We admire sports heroes who distinguish themselves on baseball diamonds, football fields, and basketball courts. We look up to stars of music, movies, and television, as well as those of business and politics. We do so because they have made it; they are successful. They have played the game and won. They are winners. They have fulfilled the expectations of the American Dream. They have realized the wealth and distinction we want so much for ourselves.

To win, we have to compete. And, in competition there are winners and there are losers. For us to win, someone else has to lose. In our focused determination to go for the gold, to excel in whatever we do, to distinguish ourselves, we often fail to realize that someone else has to lose, and no one wants to be a loser. We all want to be winners. We forget who placed second or third, whether in baseball's World Series, or in Fortune's list of the world's wealthiest person, or in elections for the presidency. Almanacs and record books list only the winners.

That's life. That's just the way it is. That's the way it is because that's what we have learned from listening to the radio, reading books and newspapers, observing other people. That's the way it is because that's what we have learned from our experience, from growing up, from being surrounded and absorbed by the American

Dream. That's the way it is because we have adopted as our own the values of wealth and distinction.

The pursuit of wealth and distinction is not new. When, in 1931, James Truslow Adams first defined the American Dream, he did so exclusively in economic terms, proclaiming that "life should be better and richer and fuller for everyone" and that we would aspire "to the fullest stature" possible.[5] Much more recently, Tim Kasser and Richard M. Ryan described the goals of the same American Dream in similar words, financial success (money), social recognition (fame), and an appealing appearance (image). Moreover, for Kasser and Ryan, it is in these terms that we determine success, for they "exemplify some of the most salient aspects of popular American culture, in which fame, money, and good looks are often portrayed as signs of one's ultimate success."[6] It's all about success, and success is contingent on wealth.

When in 1999 Ric Burns and James Sanders documented the history of New York for public television, they focused on the pursuit of wealth. New York was founded by the Dutch West India Company to make money, "to do all that... the increase of trade shall require."[7] Wealth informed the American Dream, and the American Dream informed the values upon which the city, and later, the nation were founded.

From its origins, through successive generations of entrepreneurs, into the present time, that directive to pursue wealth set the tone and pace for the city and for the rest of America. At the end of the eighteenth century, Alexander Hamilton established New York as the financial center of the newly organized United States.

---

5 James Truslow Adams, *The Epic of America* (Boston: Little, Brown, 1931), 374.
6 Tim Kasser and Richard M. Ryan, "Further Examining the American Dream: Differential Correlates of Intrinsic and Extrinsic Goals," *Personality and Social Psychology Bulletin*, 22:3, March, 1996, 280-281.
7 Dan Barry, "A Metropolis Made Great By Greed," *New York Times*, November 24, 1999, 45. See also, Ric Burns and James Sanders (with Lisa Ades), *New York: An Illustrated History* (New York: Alfred A. Knopf, 1999).

Wall Street was established in 1830, "the first time in human history that a district is devoted to the single purpose of commerce."[8] Hamilton wanted "a nation whose wealth would come not from farms, plantations, and slave labor but from cities like New York—from banking, commerce, manufactured goods, and immigrant soil."[9] The completion of the Erie Canal enabled his message to take root and spread to the rest of America. His message traveled west along with shipments of immigrants and goods to the Great Plains.

What do we want to control? We want to control others as others have controlled us. To control others, we need to be independent. To be independent, we need to have money and to distinguish ourselves from others. We need independence.

Clearly, we want independence more than anything else. That realization hits home in the ordinary experience of driving. It can be readily seen as we drive away from our homes, pull out of our driveways into the traffic of boulevards and highways, expressways and freeways, towards sure and certain objectives. As we do so, we assume autonomous individuality, and compete aggressively to meet our own goals.

In a city like New York, this dynamic becomes readily apparent because there are so many people, in so many cars, on so many roads, traveling to so many destinations, meeting so many objectives. Their numbers are so great that they appear to be conspiring to control us, to obstruct our journeys, to slow us down, to prevent us from reaching our destinations and meeting our objectives. We seem to have no recourse but to drive offensively, to assume control of the road.

---

[8] Dan Barry, 52.
[9] Dan Barry, 52.

14

We drive aggressively, weaving in and out of traffic, cutting into fast-moving lanes, displacing others, pushing others off the road, and pursuing our objectives. Why? "In much of life, people feel they don't have full control of their destiny," wrote the editors of *U.S. News & World Report* in 1997, suggesting that the automobile reflects the pursuit of personal independence and power:

> *But a car— unlike, say, a career or a spouse— responds reliably to one's wish. In automobiles, we have an increased (but false) sense of invincibility. Other drivers become dehumanized, mere appendages of a competing machine. 'You have the illusion you're alone and master, dislocated from other drivers,' says Hawaii's [traffic psychology professor, Leon] James.[10]*

Driving from Long Island, Connecticut, New Jersey, Pennsylvania, or Westchester and Rockland Counties, into Manhattan, New York drivers experience this invincibility and mastery over other drivers. They also experience the translation of that independence into competitive hostility towards other drivers, and into what has become known as "road rage."

There are several reasons for road rage. There are more cars on the road as more people are living in suburbs, adding distance between homes and businesses. The influx of immigrants accustomed to aggressive driving in their native countries— First World countries like Great Britain as well as Third World countries like Mexico— contributes to the problem. So also does the unforeseen need for more highways occasioned by the increase of women drivers; the increase of the number of cars on the road; the realization that the number of cars is growing faster than the number of people.[11]

These reasons are not, however, exhaustive. They do not explain our personal responses and reactions to the increasing number of drivers or the need for more roads. Road rage says something about us, about how we perceive ourselves, and

---

[10] Jason Vest et al, "Road Rage," *U.S. News & World Report*, June 2, 1997, 29-30.
[11] Jason Vest, 28-29.

how we act or react towards other drivers. Professor James suggests that "the real key to reducing road rage probably lies deep within each of us."[12] That is, he attributes road rage to the manner in which we identify ourselves and ascribe meaning to our lives— especially as expressed in our actions. Does our driving really identify us as invincible, as masters of our lives?

That seems to be the case, especially as reflected in our actions, in our perceptions of right and wrong. Clearly, on the highway, anything that corresponds with that sense of individual independence, of achieving our objectives and arriving at our destinations, is perceived as right, as good, as beneficial. Consistent with that individualized identity, as well as with its individualized objective, is a perception of others as creating roadblocks, as presenting obstacles, as restricting, impeding, and interfering with the realization of our own identities, our own objectives, and our own meaning. They are bad; they are evil. They are our enemies.

Not everyone on the road is a hostile and aggressive enemy. Once in awhile, someone defers to us, allowing us to enter from a side street and onto a boulevard. Once in awhile, someone moves from the left lane into the right to allow us to proceed at a faster, quicker speed. There are other examples of these kinds of courtesy and consideration, and all of them have two things in common. First, they are unusual and uncommon, even rare. Second, they reflect acquiescence and accommodation. They would surrender to us, to our own concerns and interests, to our own objectives. We like them; we are grateful to them. They are good. They are our friends.

As we have been treated, we treat others. As we have been formed and shaped, so now we form and shape others. From what we have experienced, we contribute to experience. We would have others view the world as we do. From our experience we learn, first and foremost, to set ourselves off from others, apart from

---

12 Jason Vest, 30.

others, to disconnect ourselves from others. We turn away from others and into ourselves, and we expect others to do the same.

We extend our experience of driving into all of life. We divide the world of others and the world of nature into friends and enemies. We use them or ignore them according to whether they accommodate or defer our own interests. Traveling on the highways of life, we focus on ourselves, on our own self-interests, on meeting our own objectives, and expect others to either help us or hinder us. Insofar as they do, we like them; insofar as they don't, we dislike them.

For our own independent self-interests, we divide the world of our experience. We do so out of a sense of entitlement. We have a right to what we want, especially to what it takes to achieve wealth and distinction. As people and organizations have conspired to form and shape us, to mold and program us to meet their expectations, so now it is our turn to expect of others what has been expected of us.[13]

Is that what we've learned? Is that what our experience has taught us? Are we really that focused on our own self-interests? Are we really that greedy and that selfish? Insofar as we pursue the American Dream, what else can we conclude? What else can we say?

That conclusion is unsettling and uncomfortable. As true and reflective of our experience as it may be, it is, nevertheless, disconcerting. It might even be embarrassing. We don't want to be greedy and selfish. Or, if we do, we certainly don't want others to know about it.

But, if that's the way it is, can we possibly do otherwise? Can we possibly adopt any other perspective on life in general and on life in particular? Can we be anything

---

[13] Robert J. Samuelson, "How our American Dream Unraveled," *Newsweek*, March 2, 1992, 32-39.

but greedy and selfish? Our driving seems to indicate that we can be, for as others surrender to us, we find ourselves surrendering to others.

Perhaps even more revealing about the experience of driving is how much a habit it has become, and how that habit reflects a simultaneity and consistency of active aggression and passive acquiescence. This implies that we identify ourselves as independent and dependent at the same time and in the same way. It also suggests that we pursue selfishness and greed and empathy and sacrifice at the same time and in the same way.

There is, then, in our experience not only something of both independence and dependence, but the possibility of appreciating them within an integrated synthesis fractured when we exaggerate one over the other. That experience of synthesis, then, raises the possibility of the synthesis itself becoming habitual, and of acting and reacting within that synthesis on an habitual basis.

Then, Towards Empathy and Sacrifice

There is an alternative, and that alternative arises from experience. It arises from our experience of other people and institutions. We readily see and hear that people and institutions return to others something of their wealth. Why do they do it? Is caring for others, surrendering something to those in need, simply a by-product of the pursuit of wealth?

Although Ric Burns and James Sanders focused on the pursuit of wealth as the primary driving force in the foundation and expansion of New York City, they found that it was not the only one. It was accompanied by an underlying racial, religious, and political tolerance. In Sanders' words, everyone became "equalized in the sense of: 'What can you do for me? I don't want to be your friend; let's just do business…'"[14]

Interpreted another way, the question implied tolerance and acceptance: "I don't need to be your friend. I don't care what color you are, what your religion is or what your politics are. But if you put up the cash, we'll do business."[15]

People from many cultures were accepted into the early colony, and later into the city, because they would contribute to the creation of wealth. Superiors in Holland overruled Peter Stuyvesant when he tried to banish Jews from New Amsterdam because they would contribute to the colony's wealth.[16]

Social reform also accompanied the pursuit of wealth. When, in the nineteenth century, affluent New Yorkers built town houses and mansions uptown, poor immigrants gathered downtown in rundown tenements, with unpaved roads and poor sewerage, subjected to disease and death. These extremes set the stage for social reform, and for New York's preeminent role, leading the rest of the country in the establishment of labor unions and legislation for better living and working conditions. In effect, New York introduced to all of America, according to the historian Mike Wallace, "a sense of entitlement… based on the notion that people are entitled, by their citizenship, to certain rights… to decent housing, public health, free education."[17]

This sense of entitlement arose from, and was a by-product of, the pursuit of wealth. Uneducated people, subject to disease and death, could not create or sustain

---

[14] Dan Barry, 52.
[15] Dan Barry, 52.
[16] Ric Burns and James Sanders, with Lisa Ades, 15.
[17] Dan Barry, 52.

wealth. They could not contribute to the distinction and wealth of the American Dream. For another historian, Kenneth Jackson, social reform represented a lesson from rugged capitalism: "You have to take care of people trampled along the way."[18] Care for others arose as a by-product of the pursuit of wealth and distinctions, and its inclination towards selfishness and greed. It reflected "a resistance to greed playing out" claimed yet another historian, Peter Quinn.[19]

Even today, in radio broadcasts, newspaper articles, and television commercials we hear this message from time to time: we are to care for others, especially for the losers of this world. We are to surrender something of ourselves to them, to feel for them, to have empathy and compassion for them. That care is also extended to nature. We are to hug trees and keep the lakes and rivers free from pollution. We are to preserve the fragile ecology of the world. Why? Because it is in our best interests. It is good for us.

Why would we want to? Because we feel good about contributing to those in need? We want to give back to society something of our success? We reach out to others and to nature, surrendering something of ourselves to them, having empathy and compassion for them, because it enhances and enriches us. It makes us feel good; it adds something to our stature.

It reflects our success, and the power accompanying success. We are doing so well that we can share something of our wealth. We have made it; we have won. Now, we can turn to others and give something of the hard-earned success we have acquired through our dogged pursuit of wealth and distinction. We feel good about helping others because doing so reflects our own hard-earned success.

---

[18] Dan Barry, 52.
[19] Dan Barry, 52. He also quotes the historian Daniel Czitrom: "But you still have this super-exploitation of workers in these cockroachlike industries... And you have people paying a quarter-million for one-bedroom apartments in Manhattan."

We give to others because it does something for us, because there is a return on the investment. Individuals and multi-national corporations contribute to social, educational, and artistic programs because giving boosts their images, and because it brings their names and their products into prominence. They are about wealth and distinction, and want to let others know they have achieved them to the extent that they have enough to give some away. In the world of business, we have coined a phrase for that kind of giving. We commonly refer to it as "social responsibility."

True, these people and institutions are caring for themselves, and giving something to others. There is even a question as to whether they should do so. Are not these businesses reneging on their responsibility to enhance shareholder value?[20] Are these people failing to provide their children and heirs with money due them?

There is, however, in our experience, something that says that we do not give of ourselves simply because it makes us feel good, or enhances us, or gives us something in return. Driving along highways and expressways, others defer to us, surrendering something of themselves to us. Why do they put the brakes on their objectives, and allow us to overtake them? Are they afraid that unless they do so we'll run them off the road? Are they doing so because they know, in their heart of hearts, that we'll be grateful to them? Because they know that some day someone else may do the same for them?

There is something in our experience of our families and neighbors, even of our friends and acquaintances, that people will surrender something of themselves to us simply because they love us. They will even go out of their way for us, sacrifice something of themselves for us for no apparent reason, for no apparent return. In response, we might want to question their hidden motivations. Perhaps there is

---

[20] Milton Friedman, "A Friedman Doctrine: The Social Responsibility of Business is to Increase its Profits," *New York Times Magazine*, Septmber 13, 1978, 32ff. See also Laura Pincus Hartman, "Ethics and Corporate Social Responsibility," *Perspectives in Business Ethics* (Chicago: Irwin McGraw Hill, 1998), 242-279.

some reason, but we don't see it, at least at that moment. Perhaps our parents are indirectly expressing their own expectations of us. Perhaps they are subtly reflecting their own desires that we eventually reflect them and their success as parents.

Does love always imply some hidden motivation or some fulfillment of need? Does giving of oneself necessarily imply something in it for the giver as well as for the recipient? Do care and compassion for others imply a return on some level? The root meaning of the word compassion suggests otherwise. Its original Latin derivation consists in joining the prefix com or cum meaning "with" to the word "passion" which we translate into English as "passion" which originally denoted "suffering."[21] Compassion denotes sacrifice.

As important as it is to question our own motivations as well as those of others, reflection on our experience reveals others suffering for us and surrendering to us. They voluntarily extract something from themselves to give to others. They willingly surrender and sacrifice something of themselves to benefit other people and the natural world surrounding them.

Maybe there is something in it for them, if not immediately then remotely. The fact of the matter is, there is also something in it for us. Maybe it is a by-product of the pursuit of wealth and distinction, and of one's own self-interest. The fact of the matter is, there is also something in it for us, and for the losers of the world, for social, educational, and artistic programs.

When Kasser and Ryan identify the values and objectives of the American Dream, they do not confine their list to money, fame, and image. They add another set of values: affiliation (relatedness), community feeling (helpfulness), physical fitness (health), and self-acceptance (growth).[22] Although a development of the meaning of the American Dream from the time Adams first defined it in 1931, these values have also become part and parcel of the American experience.

---

[21] Edmund S. Weiner and John Simpson, eds., *Oxford English Dictionary*.

The implication is that we do not relate to others simply on the basis of our own self-interests, or our own pursuits for independence reflected in wealth and distinction. We also relate to others on the basis of relational affiliation and communal helpfulness. Those values, too, arise from our experience and identify us as others-centered as well as self-centered, as concerned with others-interests as well as self-interest.

Others-interest, whether directed to persons or nature, also implies that there is something about us as Americans that wants to connect, and grounds that connection in surrender and compassion. We are not simply focused on ourselves, on disconnecting from others through wealth and distinction. We are also focused on others, on connecting with them through surrender and compassion. As that second dynamic is opposed to independence, we describe it in terms of dependence.

There remains the question of motivation. Why would we want to sacrifice something of ourselves, surrender something of ourselves to others? We would want to do so for no other reason than that it contributes to happiness. Kasser and Ryan imply this appreciation of happiness with respect to compassion and surrender when they list "physical fitness (health), and self-acceptance (growth)" along with "affiliation (relatedness), community feeling (helpfulness)." The association of the two is indicative of happiness as a matter of personal value and connection.

As success is pursued with respect to independence and self-interest, happiness is pursued with respect to dependence and others-interest. That, too, we learn from experience. From one perspective, that of the pursuit of wealth and distinction, we tend of define happiness as resulting from success. Success will either lead to or ensure happiness. We cannot be happy unless we're successful. However, we have encountered people who have achieved neither wealth nor distinction, but who are happy. We have also heard on the radio, or seen on television, people who have

---

[22] Tim Kasser and Richard M. Ryan, 280.

rejected the allure of wealth and distinction, and attribute their happiness to it. These are people whose lives are focused on others rather than on themselves, on giving rather than taking.

These, too, we admire. These, too, we want to imitate. These, too, we want to be like. They remind us that there is something to be said about giving, about surrendering, about suffering. What they are giving is not only themselves, but also a message. They are proclaiming the validity of pursuing values other than wealth and distinction alone. They are announcing the importance of dependence.

Kasser and Ryan suggest that the values of the American Dream enlist dependence as well as independence, and relate them to one another on an equal footing. On some level, they may be. Perhaps they could be or should be. However, our own experience, and the ways that experience has been shaped and formed by the people and organizations surrounding us, suggest that independence far outweighs dependence, and that self-interest far surpasses others-interest.

What they are implying is that, at least in the realm of possibility, independence and dependence can be appreciated as two sides of the same coin, and that the two can go hand in hand. What they are suggesting is that the two do not exist in contradiction to one another, but in opposition to one another. They would lead us in different directions, but somehow, in some way, express a convergence and unity of identification and values; that one and the same time, we can pursue wealth and distinction and surrender and compassion.

Rather than focusing on independence as a requirement for proceeding towards dependence, we see both as original, as simultaneously co-present within ourselves from our origins as well as from our motivations. Whether from nature or nurture, we experience ourselves, identify ourselves, and value ourselves as both independent and dependent.[23] We also experience, identify, and value others and the natural world as both independent and dependent.

We would not, then, ask the kinds of questions we have been asking. We would not be asking whether people give of themselves, or defer to us, because of some apparent or hidden motivation. We would not be asking whether that motivation is driven by self-interest or others-interest. We would immediately assess it as reflective of both.

This means, that at any one time and place, we identify ourselves and our values with respect to self-interest and others-interest. To do that, however, we would have to free ourselves from the ways of thinking that have organized our perceptions and assessments. We would have to look beyond conventional wisdom and its insistence on logical qualification and quantification. We would have to free ourselves from the kinds of insistence on time and place from which we have learned to separate and divide our self-interests from our others-interests.

We are no long passively sitting back listening to the radio. We're also watching television, and although television like the radio reaches out to us, it also invites us to respond to it. We are drawn into it. Television would connect with us, and have us connect with other people as well as with nature.

As television would draw us into itself, so do people and nature draw us into themselves. We want to be drawn in, to surrender something of our selves to them, even to sacrifice for them. Empathy and compassion are voluntary. So is dependence. Dependence and its virtues do not represent the involuntary response of obedience to control we have become so used to. It is, rather, a positive surrender of ourselves to other persons and to nature.

---

[23] Judith Rich Harris, *The Nurture Assumption* (New York: Free Press, 1998). "The book has two purposes: First, to dissuade you of the notion that a child's personality— what used to be called 'character'— is shaped or modified by the child's parents; and second, to give you a alternate view of how the child's personality is shaped." Harris is questioning conventional wisdom, and its bias towards nurture as more formative than nature.

Perhaps, Towards Yearning and Aspiring

How can we identify ourselves, our perspectives on others, and our values in terms other than independence and dependence? How can we possibly remove ourselves from what we have experienced as necessary for survival, as important for sustaining and maintaining ourselves? Can we even begin to conceive that there is more to life than what success and happiness afford? To do so we would have to allow free reign to our imaginations. We would have to move into fantasy, enter into a never-never land of probabilities and possibilities.

Isn't that part of our experience? Isn't there something about us that examines everything we are about and everything we possess, and reaches out for more? Even in the pursuit of wealth and distinction, we never seem to have enough. We always want more. Even in the pursuit of surrender and compassion, we never seem to do enough, to give enough.

That dynamic also belongs to the American Dream. Before New York was a colony, and before commerce and trade characterized its origins, people were lured to the New World by promises of an unspoiled paradise, a new Garden of Eden. Even today, that dynamic towards a primitive simplicity is evidenced in the "back-to-nature" movement, and freedom from the determination of the people and institutions subtly and coercively forming and shaping us.

It is a negative experience, originating in an impulse to view everything and anything we have accomplished and achieved as insufficient and inadequate. We look around, see everything we are and have, assess it as good, and still want more. Not only do we want more of what we already have, we want more than what success or happiness, or both, affords. That more cannot be satisfied by either independence or dependence.

It is also a positive experience. It propels and projects. It moves us beyond the known and the proven, into new realms of possibility. It energizes, excites, and arouses us towards the infinite. It reflects a yearning and aspiring that surpasses the possibilities of the moment, the boundaries of time and place. It also reflects something that surpasses disconnection and connection. It is a yearning and aspiring for interconnection.

That appreciation for interconnection is represented by the internet and the world wide web. Research is not limited to a number of home pages disconnected from one another, but to links connecting one to another, and interconnection with the whole of possibility and probability. Pursuing these links, with one leading to another, and to countless others, we begin to perceive the world as not only connected, but interconnected. As we move from one link to another, we move into a world interconnected into infinity, into a matrix of interconnections that transcends boundaries and limitations of time and place.

There is something else about the internet and the world wide web that is significant. Although its primary focus is on interconnection, it also enlists independence and dependence. Each home page is a self-sustaining entity in itself. Like the radio, it sends out a message. It provides information that we can use for ourselves and our own self-interests, and to encourage our own disconnected independence. Like television, each home page invites us into itself, drawing us into its verbal and graphic representations of people, places, events, into its impressions and perceptions for connected dependence.

It also assumes connections between one thing and another. Turning on our computers and accessing the web, we say that "we are connected." Our very language betrays our assumptions and our values. We want to be connected, to move outside of ourselves towards other impressions and perceptions, other people and nature. Why do we not say, "we are interconnected"? Is something holding us back from acknowledging our yearning for more?

That appreciation for interconnection reflects a third dimension of experience, and a third dimension of identity which surfaces neither in interdependence or dependence. It is *sui generis*, having its own properties in distinction from either of the alternatives we have been discussing. This third dimension we are defining with respect to interdependence.

Its distinguishing quality lies specifically in comparison and contrast to what we have proposed as the qualities of independence or dependence. It enlists its own values and its own objectives. As the values of interdependence were defined with respect to wealth and distinction, and those of dependence in terms of surrender and compassion, the values of interdependence we would ascribe to transcendence and infinity.

The internet adds a third dimension to experience, and because it accounts for independence and dependence, it would extend the convergence we discussed earlier to encompass interdependence. It would move us towards a convergence not only on the level of identity, but also on the level of values where, at one and the same time, we would pursue wealth and distinction, surrender and compassion, transcendence and infinity.[24]

Transcendence refers to timelessness and spacelessness, and to any imaginable alternative to the boundaries and limitations we ordinarily impose on ourselves and others impose on us. It continually projects us outwards, even beyond, attentiveness to other people and nature, even beyond the cosmos and the universe, even beyond space and time.

---

[24] Nicholas Negroponte, *Being Digital* (New York: Alfred A. Knopf, 1995).

The psychologist Itamar Yahalom finds an appeal to the infinite in Freud's psychology. It fact, he claims that it is an often-forgotten and ignored, yet indispensable aspect of Sigmund Freud's appreciation for personal identity. For Freud, "mutual relations and interdependencies unbroken over long stretches" reflect how "the mind works within a framework of timelessness and spacelessness."[25]

As Yahalom explains, Freud bases this insight on an awareness of the limitations of reason which identify the conclusions of the natural and social sciences as approximations. That conclusion is, however, grounded in another, the realization, even among physical scientists, "that space might be infinite." To better understand the infinite, science turns to religion: "... scientists reached out to the mystics whose concept of infinity... is deeper than deep, darker than dark, lighter than God's own crown, the invisible world waiting to be discovered."[26] For Freud, of course, infinity is a matter of natural consideration, for he denies the existence of God or the attribution of reality to a supernatural being.

Transcendence and infinity imply mystery, and also suggest that there is something in our experience which cannot be qualified nor quantified. They refer us to mystery. Mystery accompanies and reinforces interconnection. It is "a hidden or secret thing; a matter unexplained or inexplicable; something beyond human knowledge or comprehension."[27] It is not simply an absence, but a presence. It is not simply a matter of negative assessment, a matter of what we can't or don't understand or appreciate but could were we willing to invest our time and energy towards discovering or resolving. It is more a matter of positive appraisal of ourselves, of other people, of nature, of the divine which surpass limitations of any and every kind.

---

[25] Itamar Yahalom, "Infinity and the Limits of the Unconscious," *The Psychoanalytic Review*, 85:2, April, 1998, 205-206.
[26] Itamar Yahalom, 207.
[27] Edmund S. Weiner and John Simpson, eds., *Oxford English Dictionary*.

Why would we want to pursue interdependence? As interdependence reflects another dimension of our identities, and of our values, it represents that aspect of ourselves that would seek final satisfaction and contentment in something other than success or happiness, or even in the convergence of both. Rather, it would direct us towards bliss, to that form of joy we experience in transcendence and infinity, in interconnecting and interrelating.

The historian of religions Joseph Campbell describes bliss in terms of the medieval wheel of fortune:

> *In the Middle Ages, a favorite image that occurs in many, many contexts is the wheel of fortune. There's the hub of the wheel, and there is the revolving rim of the wheel. For example, if you are attached to the rim of the wheel of fortune, you will either be above going down or at the bottom coming up. But if you are at the hub, you are in the same place all the time.*[28]

In response, the television journalist Bill Moyers questions Campbell: "How would you advise somebody to tap that spring of eternal life, that bliss that is right up there?"[29] Campbell suggests that we draw from our experiences, especially from that one thing or path presented to us in those experiences which does not conform to any imposed expectation, or to any sense of what we "ought to do." Although derived from our experiences, bliss surpasses any one of them, and attunes us to transcendence and infinity, to an appreciation of the mysterious within ourselves, others and nature. It compels us to interconnections as the hub of a wheel interconnects with the many spokes of its rim.

Earlier, Campbell discussed myth and the creative imagination with Eugene Kennedy, providing an appreciation of bliss. "We are called out of bondage to our old tradition," he claims, and to the traditional ways in which we identify ourselves

---

[28] Joseph Campbell (with Bill Moyers), *The Power of Myth* (New York: Doubleday, 1988), 118.
[29] Joseph Campbell, 118.

and our perspectives on what can be seen, heard, touched, and smelled. Bliss moves us into an appreciation that "there are no horizons in space, and there can be no horizons in our own experience." Its "central demand is to surrender our exclusivity, everything that defines us over against each other."[30] It demands that we surpass the exclusivity of our own perspectives, of independence and dependence as the only terms in which we interpret experience.

Even unattached from religious faith or belief, this momentum towards transcendence and infinity can be appreciated as belonging to our experience, and also to our identities, our perspectives, and our values. That this third dimension of our experience and our values is so often ignored attests to the power of the American Dream and its overwhelming focus on wealth and distinction. The American Dream has led us to value independence not only as primary, but as dominant. Dependence is perceived as secondary, and interdependence as even more peripheral and marginal.

We often discover interdependence, and its values of transcendence and infinity, emphasized in religion or spirituality. Yet, even there, we suspect an underlying tendency to appreciate experience and identity in terms of independence and dependence alone. In the first chapter of the Book of Genesis we find confirmation for this claim. After creating the world, and man and woman, God enjoined Adam and Eve to "be fruitful and multiply, fill the earth and subdue it." His imperative directed them:

> *Be masters of the fish of the sea, the birds of heaven and all the living creatures that move on earth. God also said, 'Look, to you I give all the seed-bearing plants everywhere on the surface of the earth, and all the trees with seed-bearing fruit; this will be your food.'[31]*

---

[30] Joseph Campbell (with Eugene Kennedy), "Earthrise: The Dawning of a New Spiritual Awareness," *New York Times Magazine*, April 15, 1979, 1-5.
[31] Henry Wansbrough, ed., "The Book of Genesis," 1:28-30, *The Jerusalem Bible* (Garden City, NY: Doubleday, 1985), 18.

Masters of nature, we are to use it for ourselves, to assume independence, and to exercise control over plants and animals, to subdue the earth for our own interests. We are to focus on ourselves, on what we want for ourselves, and use other living things to satisfy ourselves. By, extension, then, we are to use all of nature for ourselves, even to make us wealthy and to distinguish ourselves. Actually, we can readily see that it is by disconnecting ourselves from other living things, that we distinguish ourselves. It is also by distinguishing ourselves that we exercise mastery over others.

In the second account of creation, in the second chapter of Genesis, we find a greater emphasis on dependence than on independence. God "planted a garden in Eden, which is in the east, and there he put the man he had fashioned."[32] Within this narrative, it becomes increasingly clear that God alone is in control, and that man is to surrender to God.

> *Yahweh God took the man and settled him in the Garden of Eden to cultivate and take care of it. Then Yahweh God gave the man this command, 'You are free to eat of all the trees in the garden. But of the tree of the knowledge of good and evil you are not to eat; for, the day you eat of that, you are doomed to die.'*[33]

Men and women are dependent. Any independence they might attain is curtailed by the threat of ultimate and final dependence— death. Only within an appreciation of dependence can one exercise any degree of freedom or independence. The emphasis of this story is on the surrender and compassion of dependence. It is expected of woman, "fashioned" from the man's rib, as well as of man. It is within the context of this emphasis, that we understand Adam's and Eve's sin of disobedience. Interpreted by the editors of the Jerusalem Bible, eating the forbidden fruit, man and woman "claim complete moral independence," and fail to recognize the person's "status as a created being."[34]

---

[32] Henry Wansbrough, ed., "The Book of Genesis," 2:8 *The Jerusalem Bible*, 18.
[33] Henry Wansbrough, ed., "The Book of Genesis," 2:15-17, *The Jerusalem Bible*, 19.
[34] Henry Wansbrough, ed., "The Book of Genesis," n. j, *The Jerusalem Bible*, 19.

The Jewish ethicist Moses Pava quotes Rabbi Joseph B. Soloveitchik's description of this double charge to Adam:

> *The community-fashioning gesture of Adam the first is... purely utilitarian and intrinsically egotistic and, as such, rules out sacrificial gestures. For Adam the second, communicating and communing are redemptive sacrificial gestures.*[35]

In the first account, Adam's sin would consist in failing to acknowledge independence, and in disobeying God's command to subdue all living things other than himself. In the second account, sin would consist in failing to acknowledge dependence. What are we to make of this? Are we to be dependent or independent?

What the authors of these two accounts are struggling with are the determinants of our own struggles to identify ourselves and our values. We experience ourselves to be both independent and dependent, to focus on our own self-interests and on others-interest. Which is to be dominant? Which is to have priority? The fact that the final redactor or editor of Genesis included both within the narrative suggests that we have to look elsewhere for an answer to our question.

Where are we to look? The immediate implication is that we look beyond both to God. The further implication is that we look more closely into our experience and into ourselves, and find there something other than the distinction between the two we experience in the American Dream. We are to acknowledge the existence of both, and also the existence of interdependence.

What we are offered, then, are three different perspectives from which to identify our experiences and ourselves. We are enjoined to pursue three different sets of values when assessing and judging our values: those of wealth and distinction, those of surrender and compassion, and those of transcendence and infinity. What we do with them is another matter. It is the matter of what it means to be a person.

---

[35] Moses Pava, *Business Ethics: A Jewish Perspective* (New York: Yeshiva University Press, 1997), 53-54.

Sources For

Chapter 1: Experiencing

For the Definitions of "experience," "compassion," and "mystery"

Edmund S. Weiner and John Simpson, eds., *Oxford English Dictionary* (Second Edition) On Compact Disc (Oxford: Oxford University Press, 1998).

For the Image of the Radio Listener

Richard R. Niebuhr, *Experiential Religion* (New York: Harper & Row, 1972).

For the Description of the American Dream and its Values

James Truslow Adams, *The Epic of America* (Boston: Little, Brown, 1931).

Tim Kasser and Richard M. Ryan, "Further Examining the American Dream: Differential Correlates of Intrinsic and Extrinsic Goals," *Personality and Social Psychology Bulletin*, 22:3, March, 1996.

Dan Barry, "A Metropolis Made Great By Greed," *New York Times*, November 24, 1999.

Ric Burns and James Sanders (with Lisa Ades), *New York: An Illustrated History* (New York: Alfred A. Knopf, 1999).

Peter Peterson, "What my Father Knew About Economics," *Facing Up: How to Rescue the Economy from Crushing Debt and Restore the American Dream* (New York: Simon & Schuster, 1993).

Robert J. Samuelson, "How our American Dream Unraveled," *Newsweek*, March 2, 1992.

For The Description of "Road Rage"

Jason Vest et al, "Road Rage," *U.S. News & World Report*, June 2, 1997.

For the Discussion of Social Responsibility

Milton Friedman, "A Friedman Doctrine: The Social Responsibility of Business is to Increase its Profits," *New York Times Magazine*, September 13, 1978.

Laura Pincus Hartman, "Ethics and Corporate Social Responsibility," *Perspectives in Business Ethics* (Chicago: Irwin McGraw Hill, 1998).

For the Discussion of Nature and Nurture

Judith Rich Harris, *The Nurture Assumption* (New York: Free Press, 1998).

For the Image of the Internet

Nicholas Negroponte, *Being Digital* (New York: Alfred A. Knopf, 1995).

For the Description of Transcendence and Infinity

Itamar Yahalom, "Infinity and the Limits of the Unconscious," *The Psychoanalytic Review*, 85:2, April, 1998.

For the Description of Bliss

Joseph Campbell (with Bill Moyers), *The Power of Myth* (New York: Doubleday, 1988).

Joseph Campbell (with Eugene Kennedy), "Earthrise: The Dawning of a New Spiritual Awareness," *New York Times Magazine*, April 15, 1979.

For the Biblical Accounts of Adam and Eve

Henry Wansbrough, ed., "The Book of Genesis," *The Jerusalem Bible* (Garden City, NY: Doubleday, 1985).

Moses Pava, *Business Ethics: A Jewish Perspective* (New York: Yeshiva University Press, 1997).

2. Dreaming

Obedient and Objectified
Consumed by Consumption
For Individual Control

All of the determining influences which exercise control over our lives can be easily assumed into one, the American Dream. It represents the totality of people and organizations which command us to obey, to buy into its expectations, to realize its objectives. The American Dream assumes a personal identity of its own, exercises determinative influence on us, demanding that we meet its expectations and its objectives.

It possesses all of the attributes of a strong, forceful person. Influencing us persuasively and coercively, directly and indirectly, obviously and subtly, the American Dream determines us through the individual persons and corporate institutions of our experience. It would want us to assume its perspective and its

37

values. We might compare it to the powerful, determining person we speak of as Mother Nature, and as we're all aware, "you can't fool Mother Nature." Neither can we ignore her or her control over us.

Neither can we escape her or her influence over our lives, over our actions and reactions. If we ignore her or fail to assess her potential for wreaking havoc in our lives, for thwarting our plans, for diverting us from our objectives, we are rendered powerless. We are reduced to submission, and to pursuing life according to her demands.

As we examine the American Dream, then, let us do so from this perspective. Let us imagine that the American Dream is a cruel master or mistress whose control over us is so determinative, and overwhelms us so forcefully and definitively that we can't begin to conceive of release or respite. Let us also imagine that we would want freedom and deliverance from its determinative influences. To accomplish that objective we will have to appreciate, first, its persuasive and coercive strength and energy; second, its demanding and exacting objectives and expectations; and, third, the need to devise or invent a way of translating its control into power for ourselves.

To effect that translation, we have to know what we're up against. We also have to know that there is a way out, and that we can assume a broader, wider, deeper perspective on life and its meaning than that afforded by the American Dream. As there is more to life than the determinative control of Mother Nature, so there is more to life than the determinative control of the American Dream.

The determinative influences of the American Dream, and its emphasis on the physical and the rational would turn us in on ourselves, to focus on ourselves rather than on other people, nature, the cosmos, or God. Any possibility of integration or synthesis is lost, and we are rendered selfish and greedy.

First defined by James Truslow Adams in 1931, the American Dream represents:

> *a land in which life should be better and richer and fuller for every man with opportunity for each according to his ability or achievement... It is not a dream of motor cars and high wages merely, but a dream of social order in which each man and each woman shall be able to attain to the fullest stature of which they are innately capable, and to be recognized by others for what they are, regardless of the fortuitous circumstances of birth or position.*[1]

Finding our attention drawn to motor cars and high wages, we readily see that the American Dream is about economics, about working for possessions, and about making the kinds of salaries which will provide us with the things we want. That's why we work. That raises another question, though. Why do we want the things we want?

The American Dream is also about reaching full potential, but here potential is confined to economic wealth and distinction. We work because we want to achieve, and because that achievement gives us a sense of purpose, a sense of usefulness. It is something to work towards. In other words, it provides us with a context in which to prove ourselves valuable and useful. More questions: Why do we have to prove ourselves? Why do we have to prove ourselves as useful? Why do we equate utility with identity?

Third, as we can readily see, the American Dream is about recognition, and about status and prestige in society. We work not only for money, but also for social status. We measure that status with respect to that of our parents, and want to have a better life than theirs, to move up a step or two on the socioeconomic ladder. Another basic question: Why do we want social status?

We identify ourselves with respect to wealth and status because we identify our-

---

[1] James Truslow Adams, *The Epic of* America (Boston: Little, Brown, 1931), 374.

selves with respect to utility and objectification.[2] The social order encouraged by the American Dream would identify us with respect to our usefulness, especially in terms of obedience. That usefulness would be measured rationally and quantitatively, numerically and mathematically. It would focus on achievement, and value those who achieve more as useful and those who achieve less as useless.

Measuring our self-worth with respect to our usefulness, we are objectified. We are objectified with respect to the objects we create, the tasks we perform, the contributions we make, the demands we meet. And, objects can be discarded when no longer useful.

Obedient and Objectified

Even more, we become so absorbed with collecting objects and performing tasks that we identify ourselves with them. Responding and reacting in obedience to the American Dream's control over us, we want to "be the best that we can be," but primarily and overwhelmingly with respect to wealth and status, and in expressing both through the objects we possess. Rarely, if ever, do we want to "be the best that we can be" with respect to surrender and compassion or transcendence and infinity.

The determining powers of the American Dream direct us towards independence. They would have us express that independence in externalities and appearances, so much so that we focus on them as the end-all and be-all of our lives.

---

[2] Amitai Etzioni, "Money, Power and Fame," *Newsweek*, September 18, 1989, 10. Etzioni uses the triad of money, power, and fame, and ties them to self-interest, to express the same perspective we are addressing with respect to wealth and distinction.

We focus on them so intently that we assess ourselves with respect to what we own. It is not only that consumerism has consumed us, but it has also consumed any meaning we might ascribe to our lives.

With this overpowering determination towards independence comes a concentration on success accompanied by the relegation of happiness and bliss to secondary status. To verify that claim, we need only assess the influences which determine and define us, and ask how much attention they have given to dependence and interdependence. In comparison to the time and energy expended on the requirements of success, we'll readily conclude that the concerns of connections and interconnections, of relationships, to one another, to nature, to the cosmos, and to God, have been minimal.

Actually, what the American Dream determines with respect to dependence and independence moves beyond secondary relegation. It subsumes them into independence, strips them of positive existence in their own right, and redefines them as by-products of independence. The American Dream seduces us into believing that there is simply nothing more to life than isolated, individual autonomy; obedience to the controlling, determining power of others— and self-interest.

The American Dream is so powerful and so determinative that it would reduce all of our relationships to self-interest. It would define them with respect to the quest for self-interest, and appreciate them only insofar as they contribute to the individual attainment of wealth and status. It would have us view others as objects to be used to satisfy our own selfishness and greed.

It is so powerful and so determinative that it would command obedience and compliance in proportion to its controlling influence. It would demand that we obey its directives to identify ourselves as things. Moreover, it would demand that we identify ourselves as mathematically determined, numbered on a scale of zero to whatever. Fundamentally, it would demand that we identify and value ourselves with respect to measured wealth and status. As we have been identified, so we identify others.

As the television producer Norman Lear suggests, we have become objectified, and, accordingly, valued quantitatively rather than qualitatively. He claims that, practically speaking, we have been reduced to numbers, so much so that "number systems have become the new currency of public values."[3] We "define our values by SAT scores, Nielsen ratings, box office grosses, public opinion polling, throw weights, cost-benefit analyses, quarterly reports, bottom lines."[4] The person is identified according to one's relative position along a statistical continuum.

The realization that we do so without questioning is, in itself, indicative of the American Dream's control over us. It is a control which pervades our identities, and which extends to our ethics, and to the ways we distinguish right from wrong. The powerful directives of the American Dream work on us so persuasively and coercively, and consume our time and attention so completely, that we forget or ignore the connecting and interconnecting dimensions of dependence and interdependence. We also forget their values.

Ethically, we become selfish and greedy. We become selfish because we focus attention on ourselves. We become greedy because we want the things we want. We forget, theoretically and practically, that others exist, and that they, too, would fulfill the American Dream's driving, motivating objectives. Actually, we can't forget, because others, too, are responding to the American Dream's demand to identify themselves as autonomous and independent. They, too, want wealth and distinction. They, too, want what we want. The problem is obvious. Everyone can't have what

---

[3] Norman Lear, "The Cathedral of Business: The Fountainhead of Values in America Today," *New Oxford Review*, April, 1993, 10.
[4] Norman Lear, 10.

he or she wants. We can't have everything we want.[5]

What does that say about our values and our ethics? Implicitly, it suggests that we perceive others as enemies, as aggressors and transgressors, encroaching into our territory, threatening to take from us what we want for ourselves, or, beating us to it. We become even more self-serving and inward focused, because of the many enemies out there seeking the same wealth and distinction that we want.

The person is, then, identified as primarily self-serving, grasping for everything within reach, operating out of some sense of entitlement: *I deserve it. I have a right to it. It's mine. I want it or need it because it is so important to my identity, to the manner in which I perceive others and nature, even God.* There is, then, a need for regulatory agencies to contain and restrain us, as well as our impulses towards wealth and distinction.

Governments, religions, and schools try to do just that by proposing general values and specific laws forcing us to curb our appetites and to temper our demands. When we hear people claiming that we need more ethics, they are usually referring to the kinds of values, principles, and laws that would restrain others than themselves. Actually, they are urging constraint and restraint on everyone but themselves. Ethics are what others need to meet our expectations.

Unfortunately, wealth and status do not lead us towards happiness. They lead us only to success and would have us believe that success leads to happiness. It doesn't. The American Dream would even have us work for success, even though it promises happiness. In popular thinking, speaking, and acting, these deeply human aspirations are pursued as synonymous or interrelated, as somehow connected to one

---

[5] Robert J. Samuelson, *The Good Life and its Discontents: The American Dream in the Age of Entitlement, 1945-1995* (New York: Random House, 1995), xxii.

another. The American Dream, especially as contextualized within business, would have us believe that happiness and success are one and the same, and that both can be realized in work.

Actually, success and happiness are two different things, but that distinction will come as a surprise to men and women whose very identity and purpose have been directed towards the American Dream and its promise of happiness and success. The formula we've become accustomed to is relatively simple: hard work will lead to success, and success to happiness. It is a formula we have been conditioned to accept and pursue. We are even to work hard at our relationships with one another, with nature and the cosmos, with our relationships with God. They don't come to us easily.

Success is everything. Aliza Rotenstein forwarded this vignette of New York life to the *New York Times*:

> *Something happened recently that made me stop for a minute and think. As I was getting off the subway at Avenue of the Americas and 23rd Street during a typical morning rush hour, the conductor said, "Have a successful day." A number of passengers smiled and commented. It struck me as somehow more meaningful than the usual "good," "nice," or "pleasant." "Successful"— whatever success implied to each individual, that was the conductor's wish. I think each subway rider who heard the announcement spent some time that morning thinking about exactly what it was they wanted from the day.*[6]

Success is something we want from the day. Not something others want. It is not something that we want for others, but for ourselves.

Happiness refers to connections, and to joining the individual person to other persons, to the natural world and the cosmic universe. We can pursue happiness only by concentrating on these connections, and by broadening and deepening our appreciation of our connections to others. Bliss, would intensify and expand these

---

[6] Enid Nemy, "Metropolitan Diary," *New York Times*, November 15, 1999, B4.

connections. It would take everything we mean by success and everything we mean by happiness, and connect them to one another. However, it would intensify and expand these connections even further, because it would also connect everything we're about to everything everyone else is about, and move even further into the realms of the probable, the possible, and the imaginable-- to the infinite possibilities represented by faith in God.

Success is focused on individual independence and isolated detachment. It is directed towards separation and distinction. Driven primarily by self-interest, it would direct the person towards self-reliance and self-sufficiency. We can pursue success only by distinguishing ourselves, and by differentiating and separating ourselves from others, the world, and God.

The American Dream, while promising both, directs us primarily towards success. It appeals to self-interest to such an extent that it denies not only happiness, but bliss as well. It ignores attention to the relational integrity of the person and the connections to other persons, to the natural world, and to the cosmic universe, and even to the interconnections of transcendence and infinity. In other words, the American Dream redefines happiness in terms of success, and translates its virtues of independence and self-reliance in such a manner that they become the virtues of happiness.

The American Dream's assumptions and objectives are so overwhelmingly driven towards success that they preclude happiness or bliss. They are so powerful that they exclude any consideration of others, of the natural world, or of God except insofar as they contribute to or deflect from success. Yet, it is in these relationships that we experience happiness.

The American Dream, however, is not interested in happiness. It is interested only in success, and to that end promotes autonomous independence, and excludes anything and everything else. The American Dream focuses on the individual, and directs that individual to conceptualize and pursue a path towards success, regardless of other people, nature, and God.

Consequently, the American Dream encourages selfishness and greed. This indictment is harsh and unqualified, but if we're honest with ourselves we'll realize just how true it is. Stepping back, retreating into ourselves, we'll also see that the origins and causes of that greed and selfishness are not of our own making, or of some inner compulsion, or even of the very "nature" of humanity. They originate in rational and philosophical assumptions and objectives as pervasive and encompassing as the air we breathe. Not only are they pervasive, they are also persuasive, seductively drawing us into their enmeshing and entangling webs.

Morally or ethically speaking, if there is one over-riding sin of American life and business today, it is the sin of failing to acknowledge the extent to which we have been drawn into the American Dream and its false hopes and empty promises. It is the sin of failing to realize just how much we have been swimming along in its current, and drawn along in its stream. It is the sin of pursuing success alone.

The American Dream is an abstraction, but its determinative influence over us is so powerful and immediate that we can practically attribute personal qualities to it. It is a commanding, authoritative person exercising power over us of such magnitude and enormity that it motivates and drives us in ways which elude awareness, and towards destinations we neither question nor challenge. It does so, moreover, for its own sake, and would direct us to fulfill its assumptions and strive for its objectives. It would have us appropriate its selfishness and greed to ourselves, and do so practically and experientially. However we would identity ourselves, or might describe ourselves, or would like to think of ourselves, becomes inconsequential when confronted by the control and power of the American Dream.

The American Dream situates selfishness and greed in an exclusive emphasis on the individual expressed by an overwhelming concentration on possessions. This emphasis on the individual is so exclusive that it relegates people to secondary, peripheral, or even unnecessary consideration. We care for others only after we have taken care of ourselves, or only insofar as they contribute to the pursuit of success. Likewise, we care for the environment, but only because of what it can do for us, and how it can help us to attain success. God— whether for Christians, Jews, Buddhists, Muslims, atheists or agnostics— is of value or interest only insofar as it aids or hampers the attainment of success.

Basically, the American Dream has deprived us of any sensibility towards a complete and comprehensive, total and integral, appreciation of ourselves as persons and the meaning and purpose we want in our lives. It does so by concentrating so intently on the person as an autonomous individual that it excludes a corresponding emphasis on the person as dependent or interdependent, and as communal and relational.

This emphasis on the individual as an object can be seen in the objectives towards which people are directed: the acquisition of possessions. Reversing the process, we find ourselves striving for things, for objects. Then, we create plans and strategies to guide and direct us towards this acquisition and possession. Focusing on ourselves as individuals, we name our objectives, strategize to meet them, and in the process become so focused on ourselves that we confuse people with things, and people become objects we want to acquire, possess, and control for our own interests. In these terms, then, we define self-fulfillment and self-satisfaction, as well as success and happiness.

We want degrees to get jobs. We want jobs to get money. We want money to get four-bedroom houses in the suburbs, with yards surrounded by an eight-foot fence, two luxury cars in the garage, and a husband or wife with children to inhabit them. Within that scenario, the spouse and the children are as much objects as the houses or cars. They, too, are objects of plans and strategies for individual success. Perhaps of greatest significance, though, is the fence, reflective of the isolated and detached individualism we so desperately seek. It images isolation and self-absorption insulating us, and our possessions, from anything and everything outside its enclosure.

The American Dream demands that we work, for how, otherwise, could we meet its objectives? Without working, how could we realize the wealth and distinction it values so highly? Not only do we work to obey its directives, but we also identify ourselves with the work that we do, the wealth we amass and the distinctions we attain. Perhaps in work, in business, more than in any other of our experiences, we identify ourselves and our ethics with respect to the American Dream. Ironically, it is in work, in business, we seek release from its control, and strive for independence through wealth and distinction.

Within this perspective, then, work is more than a career or a means of survival. It represents our identities as persons, and the meaning and purpose we ascribe to life individually and collectively. It is within this larger and broader perspective of life, and of our personal journeys towards personal identity and meaning in life, that we want to situate work. When we think about work, and about ourselves as workers, we focus intently on what we do, where we do it, and with whom and for whom we do it. Rarely, do we step back to situate that context and the expectations of people, places, and things within the whole of our lives.

We think, speak, and act, accommodating our own interests and concerns to the immediate demands of that situation, or bracketing them to focus attention on meeting the demands of job descriptions, the requirements of maintaining employment, or the prerequisites for advancing up the corporate ladder. From that perspective, rather than situating work within personal identity and meaning, we situate personal identity and meaning within work. We literally, as well as figuratively, lose ourselves in our work, and then try to convince ourselves that we're both happy and successful.

Consumed by Consumption

"At the heart of the American dream," writes journalist Cathleen McGuigan, "is home sweet home—the private sanctuary of the family, the fortress against the outside world."[7] Reporting on an architectural exhibit at the Museum of Modern Art in New York, McGuigan explains that "with more people working at home, the line between public and private arenas has blurred." Architects are designing homes without walls, or with glass walls as well as "walls made of liquid-crystal display screens for interactivity" to meet this newly-perceived need for an integrated synthesis of the individual person with other persons, and with nature and the cosmos, as well as with God. She claims, however, that:

> *Now at the millennium, we're a long way from embracing those ideals. We may live in a society where people tell all on national TV, but most of us still want to go home to a traditional house and shut the door.*[8]

Not only do we want to shut the door, we also want to shut the gates of six-foot tall fences, reflecting a drive to claim power for ourselves, to arrest the controlling influences of others, to have some space and privacy of our own. We want to retreat into ourselves.

We notice this especially in New York where people on the crowded subways, buses, and trains of the daily commute to work reflect that same need. People rarely

---

[7] Cathleen McGuigan, "Burning Down the House," *Newsweek*, July 19, 1999, 64.
[8] Cathleen McGuigan, 64.

speak to one another and become so immersed in their own newspapers, novels, and bibles that they consider any disturbance an imposition. They sense the overwhelming power and control of others, even of others like themselves, and want to claim it for themselves.

These are not the qualities and virtues we ordinarily associate with the American Dream. Yet, as we begin to unravel its underlying implications, we begin to see how it has inspired a vicious circle which has swept us into its circumference, blinding us to anything or anybody outside of its boundaries and limitations. It is the American Dream and its inherent greed and selfishness which have led us towards a myopic self-absorption so powerful that it would defer us from consideration of others. It would also defer us from consideration of the natural ecology, and from faith in God. Other people, the natural world, and even God are important only insofar as we can use them for what we want.

They have no value other than as objects which either contribute to, or deflect us from, our pursuits of wealth and distinction. Why, for example, do we pray? We pray for what we want, when we want it, the way we want it— for ourselves. As long as God responds to us favorably, we'll keep her/him. Failing to meet our needs, we discard God as we do any other object no longer useful.

We do the same with friends, who, once we have moved up the corporate ladder leaving them behind, we no longer need. "We no longer have anything in common," we might say. What we mean, however, is that they are no longer useful to us. They have not reached the same status of distinction as we have, and certainly don't earn salaries as high ours. They can no longer help us. We discard them.

We have adopted the values of autonomous independence so important to the American Dream not only because it's all we know, all we have learned, but also because we have been swept into its unrelenting current. Its current is so powerful and pervasive that it forces us to identify ourselves as objects rather than as subjects, as things rather than as persons. In other words, we are simply translating what has been done to us into what we would do to others.

The American Dream's power and control over us is so pervasive and all consuming that it overpowers us, makes demands over us, and controls us. Its plans and strategies, its principles and assumptions, have forged our own identities with respect to individual self-fulfillment, and have also led us into identifying meaning with respect to the objects we acquire. We have been bombarded by these assumptions and ideals from the moment of birth as parents, grandparents, brothers, sisters, aunts, and uncles direct and motivate us to "be somebody."

The people we meet in our neighborhoods and towns, our schools and churches, echo this same refrain. It's message is the same: swim with the tide, define a career path, distinguish yourself as an individual, and acquire as many things as you possibly can; then, you'll be successful, and once successful, you'll be happy. When parents tell us "We really don't care what you do as long as you're happy," what they really mean is "We don't care what path to success you take, as long as you make money and distinguish yourself."

In the opening lines of his short story, "Christmas Means Giving," David Sedaris expresses this perspective in a cynical, hard-hitting, but revealing manner:

For the first twelve years of our marriage Beth and I happily set the neighborhood standard for comfort and luxury. It was an established fact that we were brighter and more successful but the community seemed to accept our superiority without much complaint and life flowed on the way it should. I used to own a hedge polisher, an electric shovel, and three Rolex gas grills that stood side by side in the backyard... In effect, we weren't much different from anyone else. Christmas was a season of bounty and, to the outside world, we were just about the most bountiful people anyone could think of. We thought we were happy but that all changed on one crisp Thanksgiving day shortly after the Cottinghams arrived. [9]

---

[9] David Sedaris, "Christmas Means Giving," *Holidays on Ice* (Boston: Little, Brown, 1997), 123.

The problem with the Cottinghams was that they challenged the family identified only as "Beth and I", and began not only to accumulate more things than they, but also to do so more visibly and ostentatiously. They challenged the wealth and distinction reflected in their accumulation and possession of more things. Not only would they "keep up with the Jones'," they would surpass them. They would accumulate more things to show that they had attained a higher degree of realization of the American Dream.

For several months "Beth and I" continued to compete with the Cottinghams, adding rooms to their homes, purchasing more and more things, impressing others, saying things like "'I just paid eight thousand dollars for a pair of sandals that don't even fit me'" to which the other responded that "he himself had just paid ten thousand dollars for a single flip-flop he wouldn't wear even if it did fit him."[10] This competition moved into direct confrontation over "the most meaningful" Christmas card.

"Beth and I... normally hired a noted photographer to snap a portrait of the entire family surrounded by the gifts we had received the year before" including "the price of these gifts along with the message 'Christmas Means Giving.'" The Cottinghams "favored their card, which consisted of a Xeroxed copy of Doug and Nancy's stock portfolio."[11] Purchasing things had proven to be an insufficient reflection of their true worth, their true value, their true attainment of the American Dream. They would produce documentation to prove their greater achievement, wealth, and status. They would say it with money. They would show others their stock portfolio as an extension and expression of themselves, and of everything they were about— that is, of what was really important to them. Perhaps more important than anything else was their commitment to competition.

Competition really escalated, however, when "Beth and I" sent a "foul-smelling

---

[10] David Sedaris, 125.
[11] David Sedaris, 125-126.

beggar" away from their door empty-handed, and the Cottinghams had a photograph taken of them giving the same man a dollar.[12] As the story progresses, we find the two families engaged in competitive generosity. Who could give more? Even in their generosity, they reflected their respective self-interests. The Cottinghams' new Christmas card included the snapshot of the beggar along with the slogan "Christmas means giving." "Beth and I" became enraged:

> *That had always been our slogan and here he'd stolen it, twisting the message in an attempt to make us appear selfish. It had never been our way to give to others but I started having second thoughts when I noticed the phenomenal response the Cottinghams received on the basis of their Christmas card. Suddenly they were all anyone was talking about. Walk into any holiday party and you'd hear, "Did you see it? I think it's positively enchanting. Here these people donated money to an absolute stranger! Can you beat that? A whole dollar they gave to this vagrant person with absolutely nothing to his name. If you ask me, those Cottinghams are a couple of very brave and generous people."[13]*

Earlier, their self-interest was manifested in acquisition of material possessions; now, it was reflected in distribution of those same possessions. The story becomes more ironic, and darker, as they become as intent in their giving as they were in their acquiring. They gave their children away, then their homes, then their body parts, until nothing was left. What they really gave away was the surrender and compassion of dependence and the transcendence and infinity of interdependence to the exaggerated dominance of the wealth and distinction of independence. "Can you beat that?" was their primary objective. Only now it became a matter of attaining distinction through giving rather than through taking.

To be sure, they were fulfilling the American Dream, and investing themselves in the objectification and utility it required of them. Subsuming dependence and interdependence into independence, they could not begin to break out of the box in which they had enclosed themselves, whether with respect to acquiring or giving.

---

12 David Sedaris, 126-127.
13 David Sedaris, 127.

Their primary objective was their own success.

The autonomous independence of the American Dream also governs human behavior, and translates into individualistic moral and ethical standards. The Golden Rule would enjoin us to treat others as we would want to be treated. How do we want to be treated? Basically, fundamentally we would want to be treated according to the manner in which we perceive ourselves. Because that perception is defined in terms of acquiring wealth and distinction for ourselves, we would want other people, the whole of nature, and even God to defer to us, to acquiesce before our own expectations. It is on that basis, and in those terms, that we would be treated, i.e., in terms of our own selfishness and greed.

What we really want is control over our own lives because we have none. They have been taken from us by the American Dream, and by the people and institutions of a social order which would enslave us to its demands. That enslavement becomes apparent as each morning millions of New Yorkers crowd into the buses, subways, and trains or onto the expressways, bridges, and tunnels for the one or two hours required of travel from home to work.

Rather than enthusiasm and eagerness, their facial expressions and gestures reflect anxiety and frustration, uneasiness and discontentment. Their body language reveals pressure and tension, but not only of the momentary discomfort of the crowded highways and jammed public transports, or of the long delays caused by inadequate road or rail conditions, or of unanticipated accidents or adverse weather conditions. They are worried about getting to work, and about getting to work on time. They are also worried about meeting the demands and pressures of work, and of preparing themselves for the stress and tensions they expect to encounter throughout the day.

Their facial expressions and gestures also express response and reaction to the overwhelming social and economic forces which have conspired to control their lives and motivate them towards expectations and demands over which they are powerless. "I'd rather be sailing" and "I love Aruba" bumper stickers proclaim. They could just as easily announce "I'd rather be anywhere or doing anything other than going to work." Yet, something pushes or pulls us towards work at least five days a week, fifty or so weeks of the year. Something pushes or pulls us towards success. That something is the determinative power of the American Dream.

That control of the American Dream would force us into assuming that control for ourselves, and to do so as autonomous individuals, driven by selfishness and greed, towards the acquisition of possessions and the realization of success. The American Dream does not impose its assumptions and objectives on us directly. They are imposed on us by the many organizations and institutions of our experience, those in which we grew up, those in which we were educated, and those for which we work. It is within these institutions that the American Dream is contextualized, and in which its assumptions and principles are supported and promoted. It is these organizations which motivate and drive us towards success, even success at the cost of happiness.

Recognizing the power of the American Dream, especially as contextualized within the organizations of the social order, we also recognize the controlling influence of the organizations themselves. This means that we cannot begin to identify ourselves, or meaning and purpose for our lives, apart from them. Regardless of how hard we may try, we cannot escape their determinative power over us. Even the attempt to claim control for ourselves originates within the organization's exercise of control. It is simply reaction which, in the final analysis, reflects a personal appropriation of the assumptions and objectives of the American Dream and their determinative presence in the organizations to which we belong.

Responding and reacting to control, we want to assume it for ourselves. When we look around, open our eyes to what we're doing and what others are doing, we can readily see how men and women are doing anything they can to grasp control for themselves by distinguishing themselves, standing out from the crowd. The young woman who stands in the door of the subway distinguishes herself from others sitting or standing in the aisles by claiming her own space, and by forcing people entering or leaving to walk around her.

Claiming control over others, she would inconvenience others, forcing people to attend to her. The young man crossing the street as the light of on-coming traffic changes from red to green is so wrapped up in himself, in his own need to meet the demands imposed on him, that he is either completely oblivious of others trying to do the same, or pretending to be oblivious. He wants control for himself, to serve his own self-interests, to obey those making demands on him, that he ignores others completely, even those trying to obey the demands of others.

During the evening rush hour. a limousine was double-parked on Madison Avenue, forcing cars behind it to carefully maneuver around it to avoid traffic in the next lane. This occurrence was not so unusual, but it's vanity license plate was. Its message "LUV YA" replaced the ordinary letters and numbers of New York license plates. Who did the car love? Someone in particular? Others in general? Its driver? Itself?

We need traffic lights, and no-parking signs, then, to regulate individual self-interest. We need formal and informal subway directives to regulate the movement of large numbers of people. Men and women who ignore them are snubbing their noses not only at these normative policies, but also at the people they serve in their regulatory functions. They want to distance themselves not only from others, but also from the determinative control that dictates compliance and obedience.

They are simply reacting to the American Dream's determinative control as exercised through the institutions established to embody and implement it. Moreover, they are reacting in kind, in the same way and to the same degree to which they have been forced to comply. They would make the same demands on others that they have been subjected to. They would have others obey them as they have been forced to obey. They are reacting to obedience with obedience. To assert their own independence, they would make others obedient to them.

Because men and women have no control, and because they do not recognize the pressures and burdens demanded of them, or because they are incapable of doing anything about it, they direct their own quest for control into every area of their lives. They demand that others meet their expectations, whether in the subway door, the bust traffic of Madison Avenue, or in street-crossing zones, whether with one's friends or enemies. Dependence and interdependence are lost within the overwhelming emphasis of independence

So it goes, and continues, and grows. More influential and determinative for our identities and our values than any other are the institutions of business, the companies for which we work. The consuming and exacting demands of the American Dream, especially as reflected in the tensions and pressures of the workplace, have been characterized by Scott Adams in his popular and widely-syndicated comic strip. Every day, men and women in business recognize immediate connections between Dilbert's fate and their own. Dilbert is the "corporate everyman" relegated to a tiny cubicle, humiliated by his boss, and barraged by his company's demands. To add insult to injury, his dog, Dogbert, has become a consultant advocating a continuing series of management solutions which make Dilbert's life and work ever more difficult.[14] Dilbert is frustrated, working for the objectives of others to attain independence for himself through his own wealth and

---

[14] Scott Adams, *The Dilbert Principle* (New York: Harper Collins, 1996). See Paul J. Borowski, "Manager-Employee Relationships: Guided by Kant's Categorical Imperative or by Dilbert's Business Principle," *Journal of Business Ethics*, 17:15, November, 1998, 1623-1632.

distinction. The objectives imposed on him, as well as his own, are constantly and consistently sabotaged.

The work that we do, the jobs in which we are employed, define the parameters of our immediate experience. They also reflect boundaries and limitations imposed on us by the structures of the organizations in which we work. On a broader level, the immediate experience of work reflects the principles, ideals, and values of the American Dream which we have so readily and easily accepted, so uncritically and unreflectively adopted as our own. Although they are often discussed and analyzed— philosophically, sociologically, psychologically, and economically— they can also be analyzed in reference to our own experiences of ourselves, of our own identities, and of our own journeys towards meaningful lives.

For Individual Control

The concern at hand is whether we will continue to be determined and controlled by the powerful economic and social forces of the American Dream and its drive towards success. Will we continue to be swept along by currents over which we have no control, or will we create and invent barricading dams to curb the tide and reclaim meaning and identity for ourselves? Will we continue to work for success, and think that success will bring us happiness, or even bliss?

To reclaim our lives, we will first have to become aware of, and admit to, the pushing and pulling exercised most immediately and directly by the people and organizations which exercise control over our lives. We readily acknowledge the tension, anxiety, and frustration of ordinary, every-day experience. We do not, however, reflect as readily on their sources and origins, other than to blame the most immediate and closest perpetrator.

Doing so would lead towards acknowledging and challenging the demands and expectations imposed on us by religious, educational, and political leaders representing the organizations for which they translate thought, speech, and action into determinative influence. Powerful and coercive, they would push us towards their own expectations and agendas, and pull us away from our own, leaving us personally torn, divided, and confused.

Yet, we beg for equilibrium, especially for ourselves as we're caught up within the tensions and conflicts of personal and organizational expectations. We want to pursue our own hopes and dreams, but find ourselves restrained by the demands and expectations of the workplace and the companies for which we work. There is simply no time or energy for spouses and children, for friends and acquaintances, for God.

The demands of work have relegated them to secondary or peripheral roles in our lives. It is a battle for life, for human identity and meaning, between ourselves as persons and the organizations which employ us. It is a struggle for control of our own lives. Who controls our lives? Ourselves, or the companies for which we work?

This means that any attempt to reclaim our own lives as individual persons apart from the organizations of business is senseless and futile. As much as we would like to investigate possibilities of doing so in theoretical abstraction, experience dictates otherwise. There is simply no escape from the American Dream or from the organizations of business which contextualize and institutionalize it. This claim arises directly from experience, and from the experience of men and women working within business and its organizations.

It's only appeal to theory resides in the reflections and conclusions of casual and critical observation. These, however, are grounded in response and reaction to the experience itself. The current experience of business reflects continuity with the American Dream and with its assumptions and objectives. It would focus on success rather than happiness, translating the hope and promise of the American Dream into personal alienation and isolation, into personal discomfort and dissatisfaction.

Norman Lear argues that people once depended on the church, the family, education, and civil authority for their values. Now, these institutions and their influence have waned, and "American business has come to fill the vacuum."[15] Not only has business become the most powerful institution of the contemporary social order, it has surpassed the influence of family, education, religion and politics. He refers to Joseph Campbell's historical and architectural metaphor to ground this contention:

> *In medieval times... as one once approached a city, the tallest structure on the skyline was the church and its steeple. Subsequently, as the power and influence of the church gave way to kings and rulers, the castle dominated the skyline. Today, as one approaches a city, the most commanding structures are the skyscrapers, the cathedrals of modern business.*[16]

As the architectural structures of business dominate the skyline, their organizational assumptions and expectations dominate the social order. So powerful and pervasive has business become in our world that its influence has not only surpassed that of families, churches, schools, and governments, but embraced them within its dominating control. The implication is, of course, that business dominates

---

[15] Norman Lear, "The Cathedral of Business: The Fountainhead of Values in America Today," *New Oxford Review*, April, 1993, 7.

[16] Lear, 8. See Joseph Campbell (with Bill Moyers), *The Power of Myth* (New York: Doubleday, 1988), 95-96. Lear paraphrases Campbell: "You can tell what's informing a society by what the tallest building is. When you approach a medieval town, the cathedral is the tallest thing in the place. When you approach an eighteenth-century town, it is the political palace that's the tallest thing in the place. And when you approach a modern city, the tallest places are the office buildings, the centers of economic life."

not only the social order and its values, but also those of other organizations and institutions. It does so because it captures the ideals, principles, and values of the American Dream, and orders, structures, organizes them for itself and for us.

From Lear's perspective, we can conclude that the ideals and principles which drive business will also drive us, as well as the ways in which we identify ourselves and meaning in our lives. It is through business that we will achieve the success and happiness promised by the American Dream. It is through business, and through our work, that we will make money and achieve distinction. Work will make us successful, and success will make us happy.

The emphasis and concentration on business and work necessarily entails an accompanying relegation of the other social institutions of our experience to a secondary role. Business has become so pervasively powerful, that time and energy are deflected from all other interests and concerns. So pervasive has business become in our lives, that the determinants and requirements of work surpass families and friends, as well as our own personal growth and development. Work has become so consuming that it has overcome any relationships we might want to pursue outside of it.

Even the "quality time" we would want to dedicate to the people we love is conditioned and limited by the determinants of work. In May of 1997, *Newsweek* examined "the myth of quality time," and concluded, in the words of developmental psychologist Jeanne Brooks-Gunn, how "parents who race in the door at 7:30 p.m. and head straight for the fax machine are making it perfectly clear where their loyalties lie, and the kids are showing the scars."[17] Parents are so dedicated and devoted to their work that their children are growing up in an atmosphere which relegates them to secondary significance. Business, with its emphasis on the

---

[17] Laura Shapiro, "The Myth of Quality Time, *Newsweek*, May 12, 1997, 64.

autonomous individual, has become so powerfully pervasive that it has redefined family values and circumscribed our relationships with others, with nature, and with God.

This means that we align our own hopes and dreams with the demands and expectations of business, and accordingly redefine the organizational structures of religion, education, family, and government. It also means that we are being forced into relinquishing our own identities to business, and allowing business to take possession of us and define meaning for us. We are allowing business to identify us and define meaning for our lives.

Powerless to do otherwise, we are allowing business to represent and reflect the aspirations and expectations of the American Dream. Subtly and persuasively, business has assumed such pervasive control over our lives, that we are defining happiness and success in terms of independence, i.e., in terms of arresting control for ourselves. We have reacted to the pressures and demands of business and work by adopting their assumptions and expectations for ourselves.

Fighting fire with fire, we have become so consumed with the individualism required of business and work that we have aligned our identities with them. In other words, we are responding and reacting in the same terms, and by pursuing the same methods and determinants, from which we're seeking release. For ourselves as individuals, we are reaching for the same control exercised over us, and directing our own selfishness and greed towards its attainment and realization. We have been assumed into, and consumed by, the flames of self-interest, and, accordingly, of whatever independence we can realize for ourselves through wealth and distinction.

As others exact compliance and conformity from us, so we would exact that same control and authority over others. As we are treated as objects for someone else's benefit, so we would use others for our own benefit. Not only do we want control over our own lives, but over the lives of others, as well as over the environment surrounding us. Not only do we want that control, we identify happiness and success in its terms. We want to work to have money for what we want— and what we want, ultimately, is independence— and we want it because it affords us control for ourselves as individuals.

We would expect, then, that we would be more comfortable and content within an environment which supports and encourages these qualities, and their accompanying ethics. In her book, The Time Bind, Arlie Hochschild confirms this ascendancy of business and its expectations over the family. "For many workers," she concludes, "home and office have changed places."[18] The atmosphere of work is preferable to that of the home because it is more familiar and manageable. "Home is a frantic exercise in beat-the-clock," writes the social critic Laura Shapiro, "while work, by comparison, seems a haven for grown-up sociability, competence and relative freedom."[19] It's a haven for the individualism, rationalism, and materialism of the American Dream. It offers a false freedom precisely because work contextualizes the ideals and virtues we have inherited and adopted as our own.

These ideals and virtues, though, are so different from those required of loving and attending to spouses and children, or to friends. The context of home and family requires attention to others rather than to ourselves, to personal relationship rather than to individual acquisition. We have become so comfortable with work that we have become uncomfortable with home. We have neglected the latter to pursue the former. Becoming so swept up by work and by everything it represents, the family and home have receded into secondary significance. Because of an increasing familiarity with work and its overwhelming interplay of authority and power, we have become uncomfortable in situations requiring that we move beyond self-interest and control.

---

[18] Laura Shapiro, 54.
[19] Laura Shapiro, 64.

Why do we work? Because we want to? Because we have to? We don't ask that question very often, much less try to answer it. It is an important question because it represents the meaning and value we ascribe to our lives in ways which move beyond abstraction into practice. The work that we do is a living testimony of what we value, of what is important to us. It defines us and the ways we pursue meaning in life. What do we value? What is really important to us? In the final analysis, we value selfishness and greed, and the acquisition of possessions. That may not be what we think we value, or say we value. However, our actions speak louder than words, and we spend more time at work than we do with people we claim mean a great deal to us.

One reason we don't ask these questions or seek answers to them signals acquiescence and compliance to the overwhelming control of business over our lives. Its ideals and principles, its expectations and demands have so consumed us that we have simply accepted them as our own. Business would lead us towards individualistic self-interest for wealth and distinction. Business would have us control our own lives, and those of others, as well as nature, the cosmos, and God. It is those ideals we have adopted as our own. By defining the American Dream, we begin to realize just how foolish these categories and principles really are.

Defining the American Dream, we begin to understand not only why we work, but also that what we do and how we do it is influenced by underlying ideals, principles, and values which reach out to seize us, identify us, and define meaning for us. Not only do we see how powerful an image the American Dream has become, we also see how determinative it has become for our lives; even to the point of identifying us with the material objects and physical possessions money can buy.

What is important to us? If we ascribe to the American Dream as first defined by Adams in 1931, we'll see that the answers to our questions about work are threefold: a distinctive individuality assumed into objectification in pursuit of utility.

It is these three qualities which identify us, and which provide a context in which to pursue happiness and success. These terms are illusive, perhaps too abstract for direct apprehension and comprehension, yet the concepts they image are familiar.

They suggest not only that we're concerned about ourselves as individuals, but that it is as distinctive, self-contained individuals that we want wealth and distinction at any cost. Moreover, we define and describe happiness and success in those terms, and begin to think that everyone else does also. We assume that everyone wants good jobs with salaries to support themselves and those they love; to provide college educations for their children; to have nice homes, cars, and clothes. These objectives have become ideals, ends in themselves, to be valued and pursued for their own sake.

What we don't realize as readily is that we, too, have become objects, and of use only insofar as we can be employed by others to meet their wants and needs. We find that objectification and utility of the person deeply embedded in the American Dream. We also find it deeply rooted in the hierarchical organizational structure we take for granted.

Perhaps what we want and need are two different things. We want control, but what we really need is power, power over our own lives, over our own identities, over our own ethics. Power, however, does not arise from wealth and status. Power arises from a synthesis of the values of independence, dependence, and interdependence. It arises from surrender and compassion, *and* transcendence and infinity, *as well as* from wealth and distinction. It arises from an integrated synthesis of all three.

We may be quibbling over words, but as control has such a negative connotation, why would we want to pursue it? Why would we want to demand it of others? What we really want is power for ourselves, for our own lives. Without it, we cannot escape the vicious circle of control demanded by the American Dream.

But, we do embrace the ideals of the American Dream as our own. What are they? Asking that question, we repeat one we asked earlier: How do we define success? Peter Peterson describes his father, George Petropoulos immigrating to America from Greece with his brother Nick in 1912. Both worked on the Union Pacific Railroad. It was at work that Nick's foreman had trouble pronouncing the family name, so they both changed it to "Peterson."[20] His father "worked long, sweltering hours at a menial job no one else wanted— washing dishes in a steaming caboose kitchen." He lived frugally, saving every penny, and eventually opened his own Greek diner.

The Central Café in Kearney, Nebraska was, in Peterson's words, "distinguished not for its cuisine, but for the fact that for a full quarter of a century it stayed open twenty-four hours a day, seven days a week, 365 days a year." Making no more than $20,000 a year, George Peterson "offered food to any jobless, out-of-luck soul who approached the back door of the Central Café," and "shared what fortune he had with his family and with the rural community he left behind in Greece," buying homes for his sisters and brothers still living there, and contributing to municipal improvements in Vahlia that today the main street in the town is named for him.[21]

Successful, he cared for others, surrendering something of his hard-earned wealth for others, and doing that he achieved distinction. Throughout his life, his son claims, he was motivated by four principles: a better education for his children, attaining a higher living standard, buying a better home, and a better life "not just for his own children, but for his children's children." He equated "doing better" with the American Dream.[22]

That's all he wanted, and, as interpreted by his son, what more could he want?

---

[20] Peter Peterson, "What My Father Knew About Economics," *Facing Up: How to Rescue the Economy from Crushing Debt and Restore the American Dream* (New York: Simon and Schuster, 1993), 47.
[21] Peter Peterson, 48.
[22] Peter Peterson, 49-50.

What more could anyone want? Interestingly, Peterson never really describes his father's relationships with his wife and children, or with anyone else, other than to explain that he had compassion for the losers of his world. Nor does he say anything about his father's faith in God. Even when Peterson describes his father as an "emotional man" the driving emotion is patriotism, for he cried when he sang "God Bless America." It is clear that for both Peterson and his father, fulfilling the American Dream is what life is about. Is achieving distinction and wealth what life is about for us? Rationally? Emotionally? Spiritually?

There are alternatives, whether for the immigrant parents or for their children. We do not need to direct everything towards work, and towards the wealth and distinction it offers. We can decide, instead, to pursue the synthesis of independence, dependence, and interdependence. We can decide that we won't allow the American Dream to dictate its values to us exclusive of other values.

Of the many alternatives available to us, the most obvious is that of the pursuit of equilibrium and its underlying impetus towards integration. Dependence and interdependence are as important as independence. It is as important that we surrender ourselves to others, even if it means sacrificing long hours at work and the wealth and distinction it affords us. We need to work, but do we need to work eight or twelve or fourteen hours a day, six days a week?

When we do that we lose the opportunities of surrendering to others, especially those we care for. We lose the opportunities of enjoying nature and its beauty. We lose the opportunities of praying to God, and attuning ourselves to the infinite and the transcendent.

We do not, however, want to dismiss the need to work. We do not want to lose the opportunities it affords by placing too much emphasis on our friends or our families, or on God. Equilibrium demands attention to all three, and at the same time and in the same way.

The consistency and simultaneity of equilibrium become apparent when we begin to assess ourselves, and begin to see just how much we have exaggerated reason and ignored our hearts and minds. It is a matter of how we identify ourselves. It is a matter of how we value ourselves.

Sources For
Chapter 2: Dreaming

For the Values of the American Dream

James Truslow Adams, *The Epic of* America (Boston: Little, Brown, 1931).

Amitai Etzioni, "Money, Power and Fame," *Newsweek*, September 18, 1989.

Robert J. Samuelson, *The Good Life and its Discontents: The American Dream in the Age of Entitlement, 1945-1995* (New York: Random House, 1995).

Peter Peterson, "What My Father Knew About Economics," *Facing Up: How to Rescue the Economy from Crushing Debt and Restore the American Dream* (New York: Simon and Schuster, 1993).

For Work and the American Dream

Norman Lear, "The Cathedral of Business: The Fountainhead of Values in American Today," *New Oxford Review*, April, 1993.

Joseph Campbell (with Bill Moyers), *The Power of Myth* (New York: Doubleday, 1988).

Enid Nemy, "Metropolitan Diary," *New York Times*, November 15, 1999.

Scott Adams, *The Dilbert Principle* (New York: Harper Collins, 1996).

Paul J. Borowski, "Manager-Employee Relationships: Guided by Kant's Categorical Imperative or by Dilbert's Business Principle," *Journal of Business Ethics*, 17:15, November, 1998.

Laura Shapiro, "The Myth of Quality Time, *Newsweek*, May 12, 1997.

For Possessions and the American Dream

Cathleen McGuigan, "Burning Down the House," *Newsweek*, July 19, 1999.

David Sedaris, "Christmas Means Giving," *Holidays on Ice* (Boston: Little, Brown, 1997).

3. Identifying

Experience and Ethics
Ethics and Knowledge
Knowledge and Synthesis

What does it mean to be a person? What do I want out of life? What gives meaning to my life? What is really important to me? What is driving me, directing me, propelling me forward? What we are really seeking is ourselves, our identities as persons.

From what we have seen, our experience offers three different perspectives from which to interpret life for ourselves. We can direct it towards success, happiness, or bliss; toward independence, dependence, or interdependence. Accompanying each is a set of values which will translate those objectives and perspectives into action, and into our relationships with other people, with nature, with God. On the most basic level, it is a matter of personal identification. Adopting either of these three perspectives will identify us and our values as focused on ourselves, focused on others, or focused on an integrated totality of the whole. Adopting all three simultaneously and consistently will identify us within an integrated synthesis of all three perspectives and sets of values.

What does it mean to be a person? Consulting the dictionary, we find that the root derivations of the key words we're using refer to identity and role, but as expressed in action. Originally, person referred to "a mask used by a player," and, eventually, to the person wearing that mask, to "one who plays or performs any part." Clearly, playing a part or performing a role implies action. Identity expresses "sameness," "likeness," and "oneness," but also "over and over again" or "repeatedly," suggesting a simultaneity and consistency of action. It is, then, a question as to what we will direct our identities, our roles, and our actions.

We have the many alternatives which we have been describing. It would seem, however, that we would want to direct them towards something which will offer us more than immediate satisfaction or comfort. We would want to direct ourselves, everything it means to be a person, towards long-term and ultimate "meaning," for meaningful lives today, tomorrow, and into infinity. Meaning also refers to action, for its etymological derivation denotes that which is "possessed jointly" or "belonging equally to a number of persons," eventually representing "intention," "purpose," and "a strong inclination to do something."[1]

Realizing the connection of personal identification and meaning in action, the concrete implication is that everything we do says something about us, and about what is important to us. Everything we do also says something about how we organize our lives, and the objectives driving that organization. That "strong inclination to do something" also determines our values, our ethics.

---

[1] Edmund S. Weiner and John Simpson, eds., *Oxford English Dictionary* (Second Edition) *On Cpmpact Disc* (Oxford: Oxford University Press, 1998).

The American Dream would direct that inclination towards the pursuit of wealth and distinction first, and towards surrender and compassion second. It would ignore any inclination towards transcendence and infinity. The Dominican writer Junot Diaz expresses the implications and consequences of focusing on dependence or independence, and ignoring interdependence, in the short story "Otravida, Otravez."[2] Yasmin and Tavito are recent immigrants to New York. She manages a group of young women in a hospital laundry where "bloodstains float in the darkness." He works in a bakery and "smells of bread." They share their lives with one another, within a broader social connection to other newly-arrived Dominican immigrants. Yasmin washes Tavito's clothes at the hospital laundry, and reflects that "For a day he will smell of my job, but I know that bread is stronger than blood."

As the story unfolds, it becomes evident that Yasmin has achieved some degree of independence. She has a job, and a steady income. It also becomes apparent that the independence afforded by work and money is secondary to her. What she really wants is dependence, to surrender to Tavito, to devote herself to him completely and totally.

For Tavito, however, independence is primary. His attention to Yasmin is partial and incomplete, inadequate to meet her expectations. He works hard and saves his money rather than spending it on her. He wants a house. He also wants to continue a correspondence with Amporo, the wife he left behind in the Dominican Republic. As much as he tries to reassure Yasmin that he loves her, that he would never leave her for Amporo, she is troubled and anxious.

Eventually he buys a house. They move in together, and she is reassured, even confidant that he is changing, that he is relinquishing his independence and entering into dependence. For her, the house signals his surrender to her. He will live with her and no one else. For him, it is representative of the distinction and wealth of the

---

[2] Junot Diaz, "Otravida, Otravez," *New Yorker*, June 21 & 28, 1999, 186-193.

American Dream. A few months after moving into the house a letter from Amporo arrives, and Yasmin immediately grasps this distinction of perspective:

I am pregnant when the next one finally arrives. Sent from Tavito's old place to our new home. I pull it from the stack and stare at it. My heart is beating like it's lonely, like there's nothing else inside of me. I want to open it but I call Ana Iris instead; we haven't talked in a long time. I stare out at the bird-filled hedges while the phone rings.[3]

He can't or won't meet Yasmin's expectations. The carefree birds in the hedges contrast with the intense pain of her heart, with Tavito's independence and her dependence, with his status and wealth and with her surrender and compassion. His bread is stronger than her blood. Money is more important to him than surrender.

Yasmin and Tavito have immigrated to America from the Dominican Republic in search of the American Dream. For her, that dream is one of dependence. For him, it is one of independence. She wants a better life, but defines that better life with respect to others-interest. He wants a better life, but defines it with respect to his own self-interest. What becomes readily apparent is that in pursuing one, each of them is losing the advantages afforded by the other.

Pursuing the American Dream and having his own home and his own children with Yasmin, Tavito is basically content. He has achieved in America what he could not achieve in the Dominican Republic. However, he is not willing to relinquish his wife for Yasmin. He is unwilling to surrender to her. What is he missing out on? What is he losing?

Yasmin is neither content nor satisfied. She wants dependence, and surrender to Tavito. She also wants that of him. She wants him to focus on her rather than on himself. What is she missing out on? What is she losing?

---

[3] Junot Diaz, 193.

Neither Yasmin nor Tavito reflect any interest in pursuing interdependence. There is nothing compelling them to look beyond their own respective interests. There is nothing moving them to situate those interests within a perspective of the whole, or to understand themselves with respect to the transcendence and infinity of interconnection. What are they missing out on? What are they losing?

They are losing the opportunities afforded by interdependence, and, consequently, losing something in their relationship with one another. They are making demands on one another to satisfy their own interest, and doing so, lose the opportunities of addressing their yearning and aspiring towards that "something" other than themselves. Failing to do that, they are using one another to fulfill their own expectations. They want others to do for them what they will not do for themselves. They blame others for their own failures. Why? What are they missing? What are they losing?

To answer all of these questions we will complicate matters even further, and bring in another set of determinants to situate personal experience more directly into personal identification. We will see how independence, dependence, and interdependence correspond to an appreciation of ourselves as rational, emotional, and spiritual. We will also recommend a different way of assessing our identities and our actions. Before we do that, however, we need to understand more clearly how our experiences correspond to our values.

Experience and Ethics

What about that "strong inclination to do something"? What will I do? What can I do? Is there any truth to the common aphorisms that "I can do anything I want to do," and "I can do anything I put my mind to" and "No one can stop me from doing what I want to do"? What will happen when everyone— or at least many others— want to do the same thing, want the same job, or the same money, or the same opportunities?

A more accurate reflection of our identities arises from assessing ourselves in the present moment rather than with respect to the future: "What do I do now?" For one thing, that question divests us of any kind of wishful thinking or projections— valid or invalid— into some other time or place. It also releases us from incrementally and chronologically identifying ourselves and our values, from putting off until tomorrow what we want for ourselves today.

This directive becomes more urgent if we remember how we would influence others as we have been influenced. It has become all too easy to plan our identities in stages, focusing first on a career, then on personal relationships, then on the environment, then on God. It is too easy to establish a momentum towards the future while, at the same time, ignoring the possibilities for personal identification and personal ethics immediately available to us. Projecting ourselves into the future rather than concentrating on ourselves in the present, we divert attention from the present, and also from recognizing the implications of independence, dependence, and interdependence even now. We lose sight of the realization that we can experience success, happiness, and bliss now.

Pursuing independence alone, and defining ourselves with respect to our objectives, and our values with respect to self-interest, experience dictates that we can easily continue to do so, perhaps becoming ever more and more focused on attaining wealth and distinction as the single objective of life. Doing that, we will eventually take selfishness and greed for granted: we want what we want, when we want it, and want it for ourselves without consideration of anyone or anything else.

Alternatively, we might translate those "wants" into concern for others, and decide that what we want is what others want. "Be the best you can be" means fulfilling one's own objectives, and using whatever means at our disposal to do so. Good and evil are, accordingly, distinguished in terms of whether they contribute to, or distract from, autonomous independence for success.

Pursuing dependence alone means that we define ourselves, our objectives, and our values with respect to surrender and compassion, and become ever more accomplished at meeting the expectations of others. Whether motivated by fear or caring, "be the best you can be" translates into pleasing others, submitting to their interests and aligning our own with theirs. Good and evil are distinguished with respect to whatever corresponds or fails to correspond to wanting those kinds of connections with others for happiness.

Emphasizing interdependence alone, we identify ourselves, our objectives, and our values with respect to transcendence and infinity. We continually look beyond the immediate world of ourselves, of others and nature to commune with that aspect of ourselves which offers the satisfaction offered by bliss. "Be the best you can be" means always striving beyond the immediate to grasp the whole.

Whichever of these is first and foremost for us now will likely provide the basic perspective from which we appreciate ourselves as persons, and convert that appreciation into our actions, in the immediate future. Identity and meaning are not, then, simply matters of abstraction, but of action. Corresponding to action are ethics, and judgment and assessment of those ethics as good or bad, right or wrong. Ethics, then, are tied directly to whatever meaning we attribute to our identities as persons, as well as to the objectives towards which those identities are directed.

Ethics are more than rules of conduct and behavior arising from individuals and institutions existing apart from and outside of ourselves. The manner in which we distinguish right from wrong originates in, and is continuous with, our identities as persons, and the ways in which we relate not only to people, but to nature, as well as to God. Ethics, then, are an expression of our identities as persons, and of the meaning and significance we attribute to those identities. Ethics are continuous with self-identity, arising directly from and flowing from ourselves; flowing from the perspectives we adopt to disconnect, connect, or interconnect with whatever exists apart from ourselves.

Were we to distinguish values and ethics, we would define ethics as propositions arising from our values. Our ethics would consist in specific statements of distinction as to what is right and wrong. They would arise from our values, give specific shape and form to our values, especially as those values flow from and correspond to our identities. Rather than coming at us from people and institutions outside of ourselves, they would come from us, from our identities as persons.

To appreciate their roles in our lives, and how they reflect our identities, we question the degree to which we attend to those rules and laws of governments, religions, and businesses. Do we stop at stop signs? Everyone tells us to do so, but do we obey? We do when it suits our objectives. Rushing either to distinguish ourselves or to meet someone's expectations, we pause and drive through red lights and stop signs. Likewise, we assess cheating, stealing, and lying.

We have been told, all of our lives, that cheating is wrong. Why is it wrong? Is it wrong because it violates civil or religious legal codes? Is it wrong because it ignores lofty virtues like justice? Is it wrong because it takes something from others?

Rarely, if ever, do we recognize that cheating is wrong because it identifies us as cheaters. Yet, we seem to have no problem cheating in small things— exceeding speed limits when driving, looking on another's paper for the answers on a quiz, stealing pens or paper clips from work—because everybody does it, or because it doesn't hurt anyone, or because the consequences are minimal.

Apparently, we have no problem identifying ourselves as cheaters, speeders, or stealers. We might even gain some distinction in doing so. In a short autobiographical sketch, Elizabeth Taylor remembers attending studio school as a teenage actress, and describing it as "a nightmare" because "it really wasn't like going to school. No two kids were the same age. You couldn't even cheat or look over someone's shoulder."[4] Without cheating, school is "a nightmare" because there is little other opportunity to declare independence for oneself, or to achieve success through the attainment of distinction.

Cheating may also represent dependence, and wanting to meet the expectations of others, surrendering and sacrificing something of ourselves to others: wanting that happiness arising in caring for others, wanting to please others and do whatever we can to meet their expectations, to be happy by making others happy. From the perspective of surrender, we cheat to establish connections with others.

There seems to be no way, however, to validate cheating from a perspective focused on interdependence, and on its values of transcendence and infinity. Rather than reflective of interconnection, it signals disconnection on the broadest and widest scale imaginable. It deflects rather than contributes to bliss.

When examining our ethics, then, we are reflecting on our actions, and, ultimately on our identities as persons. Our actions not only identify us, they also identify the manner in which we perceive the respective roles we play, and the masks we wear. Cheating identifies us as either dependent or independent. It also identifies us as ignoring interdependence. When we assess and judge cheating for ourselves then, we do exactly that. We focus on our own interests, whether that interest

---

[4] Elizabeth Taylor, "The Legend," *Newsweek*, June 28, 1999, 54.

assumes the form of self-interest or others-interest. We do not focus on the interests of the whole. When do we do that?

Why would we even bother? There is nothing in the American Dream recommending that we do so. There is nothing in the American Dream compelling us to think, feel, or act in terms other than self-interest or others-interest. There is nothing to lose other than in terms of ultimate meaning and personal integration. But, because we don't perceive either life in general, or our own lives in particular, in these terms, who really cares? The only things of real significance are success and happiness.

Even in terms of implications and consequences, we situate cheating in a quest for success or happiness. So important are these objectives that we would risk the consequences of getting caught. We do not venture beyond ourselves to project the implications of our own cheating for others close to us and far from us, for the whole of humanity, or the order and organization of the universe, or our belief in "something other" than what we can immediately perceive.

Why do we cheat? More often than not, we do so because we are under so much pressure to achieve success or happiness. We cheat because we are under so much pressure to prove ourselves, to distinguish ourselves, to establish ourselves as independent. We cheat because we are under pressure to surrender and sacrifice something of ourselves for dependence. We cheat because we don't want to be exposed as disobedient. We want to be identified as obedient to the control of teachers, civil and religious authorities, employers and supervisors. Perhaps, we cheat precisely to be identified as disobedient.

Especially reflective of the overwhelming dominance of self-interest is the response of students caught cheating on a business ethics examination at San Diego State University. Teaching two sections of the same class, the professor discovered that students in the first section had provided students in the second section with answers to a multiple-choice exam. He scrambled the questions for the second section. Twenty-five of the students didn't read the questions, missed the differences between the two exams, and entered the answers they had been given.

When caught, they rationalized their cheating by blaming the professor. "I know that cheating is not right," responded one student, "but what about the teacher's responsibility?" Giving the same test to two different sections was, in another student's opinion, "negligent and stupid."[5] When we fail, we blame others, and do so to preserve our own self-interests or others-interest.

Everything we do, especially how and where we expend time and energy, how we act and react in any and all situations, is a matter of ethical concern. We don't perceive all of our actions as ethical or unethical, or assess them as right or wrong, because so many of them are habitual and routine, taken for granted. Yet, these are the very actions that identify us and reflect the meaning we attribute to life in general, and to our lives in particular. We cannot address ethics apart from our identities as persons, from the roles we play, or from the masks we wear. Neither can we address ethics apart from our actions, and the meaning implicit in those actions.

To identify ourselves is to identify our ethics. To do that, we need to stop, to step back, to assess ourselves, and to do so directly in reference to immediate experience rather than to any kind of abstract or speculative identification of what it means to be a person, or how that person distinguishes right from wrong. We need to focus on ourselves, but not only on ourselves and our own experience.

We look beyond ourselves to other people, and to their experiences, and to the manner in which they, too, identify themselves, their objectives in life, and the meaning they attribute to life. We also look at what they mean to us, and how we

---

[5] Janie Reno, "Need Someone in Creative Accounting?" *Newsweek*, May 17, 1999.

value them. We even look beyond other people, and to the many aspects of nature, to discover what they mean to us, how we value them. We look even further, towards the infinite, towards that "something other" than ourselves, people, nature, towards the divine and to what we ordinarily refer to as God.

To determine that, we need only reflect on how we expend our time and our energy. We say that our families are important to us, but we spend little time with them and expend little energy on them. We say that religion is meaningful to us, but spend little time in churches, synagogues, mosques, or temples, and expend even less energy participating in their formal services and informal programs. We may even claim that significant others are meaningful and important to us, but spend relatively few hours with them and expend relatively little energy for them.

On the other hand, we spend a great deal of time working. Most of our waking hours either go directly into work or indirectly into preparing ourselves for work, or into traveling to and from work. Were we to accurately survey our time and energy, we would readily see that most of our waking hours are devoted to work rather than to our relationships with others. We might even look back on our lives, and determine the hours, days, weeks, months, and years we have spent preparing for work through formal education and informal training. We might also look around us, and observe the time and energy our parents, our neighbors, and our friends give to their work.

Concentrating our time and energy on work, our actions reflect the extent to which we identify ourselves with respect to our jobs and our careers. Those long hours of concentration and dedication also reflect the extent to which we have bought into the American Dream and its dominant values wealth and distinction. And if we manage to extricate ourselves from pursuing those values, we readily see how little time and energy is expended in pursuit of the values of surrender and compassion or those of synthesis and transcendence.

We might also adopt an even quicker and more immediate method for determining what is meaningful and important to us. We can assess our spending habits, and determine not only what we buy, but also for whom we shop. The answers to those questions are also in keeping with the American Dream and its emphasis on autonomous and individual independence.

We spend money on ourselves, and what we determine to be important and meaningful to us. We decide what we want or need for ourselves, and also what our families, friends, acquaintances, and strangers want or need. Even when shopping for others, we are often attending to our own needs and wants, asserting our own independence.

Is our shopping perhaps really attentive to the needs of others? Surrendering, wanting to be compassionate towards others, we ask them what they want and buy that particular item, or brand, or color, or style. We can even be attentive to nature, and to contributing to its delicate balances by purchasing clothing made from natural fibers or greeting cards made from recycled paper.

We might even direct our thoughts to the greater whole, and ask whether the very act of shopping is contributing to materialism and consumerism. We may even question how shopping reflects humanity's interconnection not only with others and nature, but also with the order and organization of the universe, and the mystery underlying all of them.

A valid ethical decision will, then, focus on all three of these perspectives, as well as on the values accompanying each. How will anything I do effect myself, others and nature, the whole of experienced reality? Will it contribute or detract from my wealth and distinction, surrender and compassion of others, mystery and transcendence of the whole? How we might begin to do so is the question directing the rest of this chapter. Basically, we're arguing towards an integration and synthesis of all three perspectives, of all three sets of values. Moreover, we will propose that integration and synthesis as the basis for judgment and assessment of our actions as good or bad.

Analyzing our spending habits, we analyze ourselves and our identities as persons. Because money is a scarce resource, and because we can never have as much as we would want, we are forced into making choices. Our spending reflects those choices, and those choices reflect our ethics.

Ethics and Knowledge

There is, in economics, a basic principle which assumes that, first, choices have to be made, and second, that those choices imply rejection or negation. To choose one thing is to reject another. This is the principle of "opportunity costs" which implies not only that every choice involves deprivation, but that every choice incurs costs.[6]

The principle of opportunity costs also assumes that we will always choose the item or course of action that will yield the highest return on our investment of time, energy, and money. It also assumes that we will consider all of the possible alternatives, as well as all of the possible consequences of our choices. Another significant implication of opportunity costs is that each of the alternatives from which we choose is of value.

---

[6] Patrick Primeaux and John Stieber, "Managing Business Ethics and Opportunity Costs," *Journal of Business Ethics*, 16:8, June, 1997, 835-842. See also Patrick Primeaux and John Stieber, *Profit Maximization: The Ethical Mandate of Business* (San Francisco: Austin & Winfield, 1995).

We might even interpret the implications of opportunity-costs decision-making for the whole of our lives. Rather than concentrating on questions we can answer in terms of dollars and cents, we could concentrate on questions which refer to the quality of life— questions of personal identity and meaning; questions of values and ethics. This second set of questions also involves choices, and the won and lost opportunities those choices reflect.

There is another aspect of opportunity-cost decision-making which is probably of more significance than all of the others. Rather than evaluating the choices we make in either/or terms, we can simply appreciate the fact that the more we attend to one thing the less we will attend to another. The more we attend to our own self-interests, for example, the less we will attend to others-interest. The more time and energy we expend working, the less time and energy we expend socializing. What we do not only identifies us, but also identifies our values and our ethics, for consciously or unconsciously, the choices we make reflect and reveal what we are really about. They do so regardless of what we might like to think we are about, or even want to say we are about.

From this perspective, the claim that some action or other is ethical because "it doesn't hurt anyone else" or that it is worth pursuing "as long as others aren't hurt" is ludicrous and indefensible. Anything we do, any action we take, will hurt someone or something. It will also hurt us, because there is always a negation or rejection of other possible alternatives. That school I gain admission to, that promotion I win, that house I buy, that person I marry implies rejection of other schools, other positions, other houses, other persons for myself, and the lost opportunities they afford us.

Failure to recognize this basic dynamic within decision-making represents a failure to assess ourselves, and our identities and our ethics. It also represents a failure to assess those identities and ethics with respect to others, to nature, and to the whole of real and imagined experience. To focus on ourselves as individuals, as isolated from others— all others, including persons we don't even know, or the natural resources sustaining us, or the universal cosmos, or God— is to identify ourselves as isolated and alienated. It is also to identify us as competitive, as wanting to win, as reaching for the prize. The problem here is that there is only one winner, and to win the gold, others will have to settle for the silver, the bronze, or nothing.

The principle of opportunity costs helps us to reflect and interpret our experience. It suggests that experience assume three different forms, accompanied by three differing sets of values, and that we choose one as the basic perspective from which to assess and judge our actions. However, it also suggests another way of looking at things. Rather than choosing one over the others, opportunity-cost decision making leads us to consider all three integrated into a synthesis. To pursue one or the other of the perspectives we have been describing would not only reduce the others to secondary significance, but also violate the integrated synthesis of all three, and also of the person.

When we refer to experience, we are referring to independence and distinction, *and to* dependence and surrender, *and to* interdependence and transcendence. To this point we have been discussing them in isolation from one another. Now, we are turning our attention to a convergence of all three. The sociologist and novelist, Andrew Greeley, describes experience from this perspective of integration and convergence, and in doing so recommends that we understand knowledge as originally metaphorical rather than propositional. He claims that we know ourselves first as "a scanner that collects images from the outside world" such that "the self spontaneously decides that A is like B and like thousands of other images too."[7]

He writes of an "agent intellect" that scans "the warmth and light of the fire and transiently juxtaposes it with the image of the sun." It is only then that what he

---

[7] Andrew M. Greeley, "The Catholic Imagination of Bruce Springsteen," *America*, February 6, 1988, 111.

calls the "cognitive self" takes over to claim "that both are forms of light," ascribing the properties of light to propositions to define light as distinct from darkness. Knowledge is integral and metaphorical before it is distinguishable and propositional.[8]

Metaphor integrates. Proposition separates. Not only does metaphor integrate, but it also reflects similarities that cannot be accommodated by the distinctions and categories of propositions. In the words of Wayne Koestenbaurm, metaphor urges us "to compare unlike things, to yoke incommensurables together." It is "the desire to be wrong: wrong-minded, wrong-tongued; the craving to avoid literality and law."[9] Greeley and Koestenbaum are suggesting that there exist at least two levels of experience, and that the two differ fundamentally. The basic difference resides in the realization that something is lost as we move from one to the other. What is lost is a sense of the integrated person.

First, we experience ourselves as integrated and unified, as simultaneously independent, dependent, and interdependent. Second, we distinguish the three, and, on the basis of those distinctions, focus our attention on one or the other, and direct all of our energies towards its actualization. We assume this distinction, and also assume that we have to pursue independence, dependence, or interdependence. We assume that we have to choose whether to concentrate on ourselves, others, or the whole. On the basis of that choice, we distinguish goodness from evil.

Choosing to pursue our own self-interests, independence becomes the primary motivating objective and the basic perspective from which we assess ourselves and our actions. It becomes the basic criterion from which we judge good and evil. Anything contributing to our pursuit of independence is judged to be good; anything deflecting or obstructing it, evil. Choosing to concentrate our attention on others

[8] Greeley, 111.
[9] Wayne Koestenbaum, "Obscenity, a Celebration," *New York Times Magazine*, May 21, 1995, 47.

and nature, dependence becomes the primary motivating objective and the basic criterion from which to distinguish good from evil. Whatever benefits other people and nature is considered good; whatever denigrates them is evil. The same dynamic holds with respect to concentrating attention on the whole of interdependence, and to distinguishing good and evil. Choosing to direct our attention to the transcendent, infinite whole, interdependence becomes the basis for assessment and judgment.

For Greely, however, this valuation of ourselves and our ethics reflects the second level of knowledge. On that second level, we qualify, categorize, classify, pigeonhole, and quantify life itself and every dimension of life. The basic differences of independence, dependence, or interdependence reflect that kind of division and separation within ourselves, and recommend even further partition and categorization of every aspect of our lives. It also recommends identification of these many differences into clean, neat propositions or statements reflective of knowledge, intelligence, and understanding.

The underlying concern, then, is whether we will choose to pursue one set of values rather than another. To pursue one, we'll lose the others, or, to emphasize one set of values, we'll relegate the others to secondary significance. However, from a perspective of integrated synthesis, to pursue any one of them in isolation of the others would violate even the possibility of striving towards or achieving synthesis.

It is this second level of knowledge, especially knowledge of ourselves, that has been reduced to reason, and to the categories and principles of rational, logical propositions. On the level of reflection, the second level of experience, self-knowledge has become equated with reason. This identification of knowledge with the dictates of rational conceptualization is reductive because it assumes that personal knowledge, personal self-identity, and personal ethics are matters of reason alone. However, experience reveals that we are not simply rational. There is also something about us that is physical; something about us that is emotional; something about us that is spiritual. We know ourselves, experience ourselves, to have bodies, hearts, and souls as well as minds.

The experience of our acting, of our doing, reveals self-identity and self-knowledge to have rational, spiritual, and emotional dimensions. There are, of course, times and places, where one will dominate the others, but, even then, none of our actions are governed purely by the mind, the heart, the soul, or the body. To appreciate not only the interaction of all four for a totality of identify and knowledge, we need first to appreciate the distinctive contributions of each.

The mind has its own attributes, separate and distinct from those of the heart and the soul. For the dictionary, the mind is, first, "the faculty of memory," and "that which is remembered of (a person or thing)." It is also "that which a person thinks about any subject or question; one's view, judgement, or opinion." Those views, judgements, or opinions are, however, conditioned by inclination and disposition: "to be strongly disposed or inclined," and "to desire to attain or accomplish."[10] We readily see that the mind is directed towards clearly defined objectives, and assumes the establishment of rational, logical steps leading towards their attainment or accomplishment.

The question, then, becomes that of identifying those objectives. Do we direct reason and logic towards independence, dependence, or interdependence? There is something about the mind, and about its capacity for reason that turns in on itself, that is directed towards independence, more than towards dependence or interdependence. That focus becomes apparent when we understand its capacity for reason, and appreciate its tendency towards rationality. Reason, as defined by the *Oxford English Dictionary*, is "that intellectual power or faculty... which is ordinarily employed in adapting thought or action to some end." More specifically, it is "a fact or circumstance forming... a ground or motive leading... a person to adopt or reject

---

[10] Edmund S. Weiner and John Simpson, *Oxford English Dictionary*.

some course of action or procedure, belief, etc."[11] Reason is, then, not only the basis for motivation, but also for action. That which is attributed to reason, that which is rational about us, motivates us towards objectives, especially with respect to action.

It is often assumed that the mind and its capacity for reason dominate not only our thoughts, but our actions as well. Driving on the expressways and byways of our lives, reason provides motivation, objective, as well as the logical progression from thought to achievement, from potential into action. The assumed domination of reason would, accordingly, carry the physical along with it.

The body would simply adhere and conform to the dictates of reason. We get into our cars, drive them into traffic with a clear destination and a clear plan of action to reach it. Our own bodies, as well as that of the car, and those of other people and other cars, impose limits and conditions on that drive from motivation to destination. The body, along with all of the physical and material aspects of our experience, however, exhibits tendencies which cannot be subjected to reason in any absolute sense. As much as our minds would have us remain awake and attentive to driving, the body imposes its own demand for sleep, perhaps causing us to lose control, to swerve off the road or into oncoming traffic. There is, then, something about the body that will not, or cannot, conform to reason. At times, it seems to meet the demands of the emotions more than those of reason.

Together, the body and the mind would dictate a perspective of self-interested independence. They correspond to interdependence and its focus on autonomy and individuality. They assume an inward-focused attunement to oneself before anyone or anything else.

Driving us, however, and playing active roles in our actions— and, accordingly, in our identities and our ethics— are our hearts and our souls. These, too, have

---

[11] Edmund S. Weiner and John Simpson, *Oxford English Dictionary*.

attributes of their own which cannot be limited or circumscribed by the rational and the physical. As false as it would be to claim "mind over matter," it would be equally false to claim "mind over emotion" or "mind over faith." Familiar with the physical and the rational, and with an appreciation of their overwhelming dominance for identifying us and our actions, we also need to appreciate the emotional and the spiritual dimensions of the person. Basically, the emotional and the spiritual direct us towards awareness of, and attunement to, others. The emotional heart represents relationships with other people and with nature. The spiritual soul represents relationship with God, with that "something more" or "something other" than ourselves, other persons, and nature.

To understand and appreciate the spiritual, we turn to the insights of the television producer Norman Lear who identifies the spiritual with respect to a "mysterious inner life, the fertile invisible realm that is the wellspring for our species' creativity and morality."[12] Having created Archie Bunker, Mary Hartman, and George Jefferson, Lear finds them so attuned to the physical and the rational dimensions of their lives that they ignore the spiritual:

> It is that portion of ourselves that impels us to create art and literature, and study ethics, philosophy, and history. It is that portion of our being that gives rise to our sense of awe and wonder and longing for truth, beauty, and a higher order of meaning. For want of a better term, one could call it the spirit-led or spiritual life of our species.[13]

Not only is that "spirit-led or spiritual life of our species" attributed to being, i.e., to our identities as persons, it is also described as "the gift with which all humankind has been endowed: the capacity for awe and wonder and mystery, the search for higher meaning, the capacity to feel the rapture of being alive."[14]

Lear's description of the spiritual is confirmed by the dictionary. Basic to the

---

[12] Norman Lear, "The Cathedral of Business: The Fountainhead of Values in American Today," *New Oxford Review*, April, 1993, 12.
[13] Norman Lear, 12.

Oxford English Dictionary's definition of spiritual is contrast or opposition to the physical or the material. It is, "immaterial... pertaining to, consisting of, spirit... of the nature of a spirit or incorporeal supernatural essence." Whatever the spiritual is, it is not physical. Neither is it rational, although often identified as a projection of the rational into transcendence and infinity.

The dictionary assumes that false and misleading assumption when it defines soul as "the principle of thought and action" and as "the vital, sensitive, or rational principle in plants, animals, or human beings" and even as a "high development of the mental faculties."[15] However, were the spiritual to be defined in contrast to the rational, or the soul as having existence of its own as separate from the mind, we would have to define its attributes.

To begin with, let us assume that whatever is of the mind, of its rational attributes, is not of the soul or of its spiritual attributes. The soul is not the mind; nor does it function like the mind. It cannot be subjected to logic, and to the same kinds of progression towards actualization that we attribute to rational thought. It has its own identity and its own function within the person. Its role is to move beyond, towards otherness, towards unimagined possibilities, towards an appreciation for the transcendent and the infinite.

To define the spiritual with respect to the rational, we would have to qualify and circumscribe those possibilities to the limitations of human thought. Pursing that path, we would lose any sense that there exists more to our lives, and to our experiences of life, than is immediately available to us through our physical and rational attributes. We would lose any sense that there is more to life than that which can be scientifically proven or verified. We would lose that "capacity for awe and wonder and mystery" of which Lear writes, and which propels us towards the

---

[14] Norman Lear, 12.
[15] Edmund S. Weiner and John Simpson, *Oxford English Dictionary.*

transcendent and the infinite. That is, the soul moves us out of ourselves, out of our own pursuit of independent self-interest or dependent altruism, towards the interconnections and interrelationships of interdependence.

Another consequence of an identification of the spiritual with the rational would be the kind of mental gymnastics which require us to rank the basic dimensions of our knowing, to qualify and quantify them with mathematical precision. We would search for ways to identify ourselves as spiritual first, rational second, emotional third, and physical fourth, or vice-versa. We might also be compelled to rank God first, and to appreciate everything as somehow subject to, or embraced by, God. We might also be compelled to identify God as having the same attributes as human persons, although to a superlative degree.

The spiritual is also defined with respect to the emotional, and the soul as "the seat of the emotions, feelings, or sentiments; the emotional part of man's nature." The emotional is not the same as the spiritual, however; nor can we equate the heart with the soul. The realization that we so often do is indicative of the absence of the spiritual within our own identities, our own perspectives on others, and our ethics.

To describe the emotional, we turn to Harvard University's Daniel Goleman and his insights into "emotional intelligence." "Emotional intelligence "may seem an oxymoron," writes Craig Lambert, "since our society has long associated intelligence purely with intellect, analysis, rationality—the cerebral capacities measured by IQ tests and the Scholastic Aptitude Test."[16]

As emotions refer to feelings, Goleman claims that feelings reflect their own kind of "intelligence" distinct from rational intelligence. Awareness of our own feelings, "joy, hurt, anger, sadness, jealousy," to name a few, "enables us to perceive the feelings of others accurately—to be empathetic, to feel with another person."[17] Because empathy "underlies many interpersonal aptitudes like teamwork, persuasion, and leadership...[it] forges emotional connection, and so tends to bond people together even more deeply than shared beliefs and ideas."[18]

For the *Oxford English Dictionary*, the heart is—in addition to "a playing card" or "the hollow muscular... organ which... keeps up the circulation of the blood in the vascular system of an animal"—"the seat of the emotions" representing "sensibility or tenderness for others." It is also defined as "the seat of the mental or intellectual faculties" and as "the seat... of the soul." Rather than defining the heart with respect to the mind or the soul, we are defining it as an entity unto itself, with its own emotional attributes. The etymological meaning of emotion, as explained by the dictionary, represents "a moving out, migration, transference... ."[19] The emotional dimension of the person moves out from the person, towards other people and nature.

It differs from the mind and the body, and their respective tendencies to move inward, precisely in its tendency to move outward. It differs from the soul in that its tendency to move outward is limited and circumscribed by the degree of its movement. It moves only towards other people, nature, and the cosmos. It does not venture beyond the cosmos towards the infinite and the unimaginable.

These definitions lead us to question ourselves even further. Are we primarily physical, or primarily rational, or primarily emotional, or primarily spiritual? At any given moment, within any activity, we experience ourselves more as one than the

---

[16] Craig Lambert, "The Emotional Path to Success," *Harvard Magazine*, September-October, 1998, 62. In addition to this interview, see also Daniel Goleman, *Emotional Intelligence* (New York: Bantam Books, 1997) and *Working with Emotional Intelligence* (New York: Bantam Books, 1998.
[17] Craig Lambert, 62.
[18] Craig Lambert, 61.
[19] Edmund S. Weiner and John Simpson, eds., *Oxford Egnlish Dictionary*.

others. Playing basketball, we emphasize the physical. Working crossword puzzles, the focus is on the rational. Inspired by a magnificent sunset, the emotional is emphasized. Praying, we concentrate on the spiritual. However, were we to analyze our experiences, study our actions, we would recognize the interactive presence of all four at any given moment, or in any given situation. We would recognize the simultaneous presence of the physical, the rational, the emotional, and the spiritual, in all of our thoughts, speech, and actions. We would experience the simultaneous presence of the body, the mind, the heart, and the soul within our very identities as persons, and within our ethics.

Assessing our actions, we can readily see that Greeley's description of knowledge as unified and integrated before it is separated and divided is confirmed in experience. Now, it becomes a matter of recognizing and acknowledging that integration, of bringing it into consciousness and into action. This would mean that not only that we are integrated before we are divided, but that we want to identify ourselves with respect to integration, and express it in our actions. Otherwise, we focus on one dimension or other of the total person, reducing the other dimensions to secondary or peripheral consideration. Failing to grant the physical, the rational, the emotional, and the spiritual equal significance, we identify ourselves with respect to one part or other of the whole. Not only do we express ourselves as partial and inadequate, so also do we assess our ethics, our valuations of good and evil, partially and inadequately.

Knowledge and Synthesis

Can that recognition and acknowledgment of the totality, of the integrated synthesis, become actualized in action? Can we actually begin to identify ourselves and our ethics with respect to integrated synthesis? That possibility becomes actualized when we discover that people like Dr. Mahmet Oz approach surgery by appealing not only to the physical and the rational, but also to the spiritual and the emotional.

An educated expert in medical science and the rational and physical determinants of healing, Dr. Oz moves beyond traditional surgical procedures by introducing music into the operating room to calm the emotional fears and anxieties of his patients. Accompanying him in surgery at New York's Columbia-Presbyterian Medical Center are not only doctors and nurses, but also women who pray over the patient through an imposition of hands: "In this ultimate theater of scientific medicine, the women were using their hands as kings once did to treat subjects with scrofula and as Jesus is said to have done and as shamans and mothers and Chinese qi-gong practitioners still do."[20]

Why would Dr. Oz introduce prayer and music into the operating room? The answer is simple. It works. Patients heal faster. However, like most medical procedures which "have at least some footing in science, and have been proved safe and effective by quantifiable standards," the role of prayer and music in surgery cannot be proven or validated by quantifiable standards based in rational principles.[21]

There is more to healing than the interplay between the rational and the physical. There is also the interplay between the spiritual and the emotional, along with the rational and the physical, even though the former cannot be verified by the same standards as the former. That realization, however, does not render the emotional and the spiritual any less important for healing, or for an appreciation of self-identity. Perhaps medical science has simply exaggerated the rational and the

---

[20] Chip Brown, "The Experiments of Dr. Oz," *New York Times Magazine*, July 30, 1995, 21.
[21] Chip Brown, 21-22. "That's the kind of test most therapies in the realm of alternative medicine can't pass. While many therapies seem harmless enough, they are often premised on metaphysical philosophies beyond the scope of science, and their claims of efficacy are supported by testimonials, not controlled studies."

physical, and, in doing so, relegated the emotional and the spiritual to the periphery. Even further, it has relegated the heart and the soul to oblivion, ignoring them as inconsequential.

Implicitly, Dr. Oz is challenging any attempt to define knowledge with respect to the rational alone. Doing so, he has questioned the very principles on which the scientific method is based. There is more to knowledge than what can be seen, touched, heard, smelled, or tasted. There is more to knowledge than that which can be observed and then translated into the universal propositions and objective principles of empirical philosophy, especially as these have been adopted by the natural sciences to determine truth and reality.

Knowledge encompasses more than the rational. It also encompasses the heart and the soul. Even though the emotional and spiritual dimensions of that knowledge cannot be verified by the same principles governing the mind it does not mean that they are illusions or fantasies, insignificant for knowledge in general, or self-knowledge in particular. Rather, they exhibit their own criteria for validation which are very different from those of the mind and the body.

Yet, to ignore or deny their very existence is to discount or neglect half of the determinants of self-knowledge and personal identity. It is to deny that the person is more than a rational animal. It is also to deny that the spiritual soul and the emotional heart play a role in assessing good and evil.

Implicit in Dr. Oz's surgical practice is recognition that knowledge is not a matter of the mind, the soul, or the heart alone. It is a matter of acknowledging and appreciating the integration of all three in relation to one another. There is more to scientific medicine than what can be induced or deduced from reason or from biology, physics chemistry and the other physical sciences. There is also more to ourselves than the mind. There is also the heart and the soul, the emotional and the spiritual.

However, when that original unity of knowledge is translated into reflection, and then from reflection into our lives with others, the mind, heart, and soul become disconnected from one another. The physical and the rational are abstracted from the totality of the person and from its encounters with others. Not only abstracted, they are attributed with overwhelming and exaggerated validity. The emotional and the spiritual are removed from centrality and relegated to the periphery. So also is independence abstracted and attributed with overwhelming and exaggerated validity to the neglect of the emotional and the spiritual and of dependence and surrender.

What has really happened is that dependence and interdependence have been assumed into independence. They have been detached from their emotional and spiritual grounding, and redefined to meet the objectives and expectations of the rational. The integrated synthesis and totality of experience has been sabotaged and perverted to define dependence and interdependence with respect to the rational rather than the spiritual and the emotional. Dependence has become simply the expected response to the independence of others. For others to be independent, others are to surrender, to be dependent. The immediate, concrete experience of integration is perverted and subverted by the dominance of the rational.

Insofar as the rational is inward-directed, its reflection in the desire for independence becomes evident. The great sin, the great evil would be any momentum towards dependence or interdependence, and accordingly, anything that would focus on the interests of others before our own— whether those of other people, nature, or God. In terms of opportunity costs, this one-dimensional perspective would necessarily result in the costs associated with the lost opportunities afforded by the spiritual and the emotional dimensions of our lives. Those lost opportunities would become readily manifested in our actions, and in our determination of good and evil.

However, were we to focus on others, and concentrate on that part of our identities directed towards others, we would become so absorbed in surrender and compassion that sin and evil would be designated with respect to independence and interdependence. In that case, failure to attend to our own self-interests would result in the lost opportunities resulting from repression of the rational.

Also lost would be any appreciation for that "something other" than ourselves and others. Yet, to focus on transcendence and infinity, we would lose a concomitant appreciation for the rational and the emotional. So absorbed would we be by the spiritual, we would lose sight of caring for ourselves and others in the immediacy of our lives.

From an ethical perspective, this integrated totality of the mind, heart, and soul would recommend attention to the urgings and attributes of each in decision-making of any kind. The assessment of any action as right or wrong would involve implications and consequences attached to all four. That is, we would assess all of our actions with respect to each of these dimensions of the total person, as well as with respect to the manner in which they interact to achieve an integrated synthesis. To do any less would reflect not only a partial and inadequate self-identity, but also partial and inadequate ethical decision-making.

It would follow then, that insofar as we fail to realize that integrated synthesis, we fail to realize self-identity and self-knowledge. Insofar as the physical, the rational, the emotional, or the spiritual attributes is ignored, so are their respective contributions to ethical decision-making. Arising from a consistency of knowledge, identity, and action, our own ethics are valid to the extent that they are informed by the whole of our experience, and invalid to the extent that they are not.

Another important determinant of the continuum of knowledge, identity, activity, and ethics is the scope of reference for their integrated synthesis. Do we focus only on our own needs and wants, or only on the interests of others, on the concerns of nature and the cosmos, on the implications of faith in God? The integrated synthesis of body, heart, soul, and mind would refer to an integrated synthesis of our own existences and well as of everything and anything that exists outside of ourselves. This means that in making decisions for ourselves, we would want to assess the implications of those decisions for others, for nature, for the cosmos, and for the divine.

At the very least, this appreciation of integrated synthesis would enjoin us to account for every dimension of the total person and every aspect of experienced reality in ethical decision-making. We would want to acknowledge the unity of the whole before its division into parts. We would want to direct our focus to the first rather than to the second level of knowledge and experience.

Only secondarily, is knowledge broken into its constituent parts. Internally, it would distinguish the rational mind from the physical body, the emotional heart from the spiritual soul, and one from the other. Externally, it would define other persons, nature, the cosmos, and God as isolated and separated from one another. It would define and distinguish knowledge itself, and the way we know ourselves in relation to what exists outside of ourselves. Connections would fade into distinctions as comparisons move into categories, and categories into propositions, and propositions into principles, and principles into laws explaining more how we are disconnected than connected.

Moving from integrated synthesis into reflection, we begin to distinguish and separate. We focus on one or the other, leaving the others behind, ignoring or repressing them if not for the moment, for the whole of our lives. For the most part, we find ourselves attuned to the rational and the physical, ignoring the emotional and the spiritual, or subsuming them into the dictates of the rational and the physical. Our rational minds and physical bodies assume prominence. We revel in the sights and sounds, the touches and smells of our sense perceptions. We marvel at the laws of nature that govern them. We might even direct our attention to understanding the ways in which the mind connects with the body, and how they come together to identify us, but do so with respect to universal and objective laws of weight, motion, and resistance.

Concentration on the rational with the physical to the exclusion of the spiritual and the emotional, then, lead us to associate identity with quantification and qualification— especially as expressed in numbers which are added, subtracted, multiplied, and divided to yield superlative categories of most and least and of best and worst, and comparative categories of more and less and of better and worse. These same measurements, coupled with the laws of nature, govern not only our sense perceptions, but the ways in which we perceive them, the ways in which we translate them into measured categories of reason, and the formulation of these measured categories into patterns of thought, speech, and action. So we identify ourselves numerically and mathematically, and assess ourselves with respect to measured categories of the body and the mind.

This underlying commitment to universal and objective laws of nature becomes the basis for identifying ourselves, the meaning we attribute to life, and assessment of ethical right and wrong. On this secondary level of experience, everything and everyone is assessed and evaluated according to law. These laws govern our identities as persons; our perceptions of others, of nature, of the cosmos, of the infinite. We assume this formalistic, legalistic stance towards life, and establish identity, significance, and appropriate behavior according to it.

Never do we ask whether this is what identity and ethics are really about. Rather, we question the extent to which we are meeting the expectations and demands of others. Never do we ask whether they are valid and appropriate. We assume they are, and measure ourselves accordingly. As measurement refers to numbers, we assess ourselves primarily in numerical terms, with our thoughts and actions referred to comparisons and contrasts with others. That is, we become obsessed with determining our rights and privileges, as opposed to those of others.

We become consumed with establishing ourselves in opposition to everything and everyone else.

That is the hidden message of the American Dream. That is also the hidden cost of failing to attend to the emotional heart and the spiritual soul. It is the hidden cost of pursuing wealth and distinction alone, the lost opportunities of ignoring not only emotional surrender and compassion and spiritual transcendence and infinity. It is also reflective of the lost opportunities of ignoring the integrated synthesis of the total person. That is, the opportunity to value ourselves with respect to wealth and distinction costs us the opportunities to do so in other terms as well.

Sources For
Chapter 3: Identifying

For the Definitions of "person," "meaning," "mind," "reason," "body," "spiritual," "soul," "heart," "emotion."

Edmund S. Weiner and John Simpson, eds., *Oxford English Dictionary* (Second Edition) *On Compact Disc* (Oxford: Oxford University Press, 1998).

For the Short Story, "Otravida, Otravez"

Junot Diaz, "Otravida, Otravez," *New Yorker,* June 21 & 28, 1999.

For the Quote from Elizabeth Taylor

Elizabeth Taylor, "The Legend," *Newsweek,* June 28, 1999.

For the Discussion of Cheating

Janie Reno, "Need Someone in Creative Accounting?" *Newsweek,* May 17, 1999.

For the Discussion of Opportunity Costs

Patrick Primeaux and John Stieber, "Managing Business Ethics and Opportunity Costs," *Journal of Business Ethics,* 16:8, June, 1997.

Patrick Primeaux and John Stieber, *Profit Maximization: The Ethical Mandate of Business* (San Francisco: Austin & Winfield, 1995).

For the Description of Knowledge

Andrew M. Greeley, "The Catholic Imagination of Bruce Springsteen," *America*, February 6, 1988.

Wayne Koestenbaum, "Obscenity, a Celebration," *New York Times Magazine*, May 21, 1995.

For the Description of the Spiritual

Norman Lear, "The Cathedral of Business: The Fountainhead of Values in America Today," *New Oxford Review*, April, 1993.

For the Description of the Emotional

Craig Lambert, "The Emotional Path to Success," *Harvard Magazine*, September-October, 1998.

Daniel Goleman, *Emotional Intelligence* (New York: Bantam Books, 1997) and *Working with Emotional Intelligence* (New York: Bantam Books, 1998).

For Dr. Oz's Experiment

Chip Brown, "The Experiments of Dr. Oz," *New York Times Magazine*, July 30, 1995.

4. Valuing

Ignatius J. Reilly
Value and Perception
Perception and Identity
Identity and Synthesis

The American Dream would have us pursue success, and would also have us relegate happiness to secondary importance, and ignore bliss altogether. To be the "best we can be" we want to pursue success, happiness, and bliss. Moreover, we want to pursue all three within an integrated synthesis wherein all three are consistently and simultaneously present at any given moment and in any given time or place. We want to identify ourselves as rationally disconnected, emotionally connected, and spiritually interconnected, and also assume a perspective on others reflective of independence, dependence, and interdependence. To do otherwise would result in partial and inadequate identities for ourselves, perspectives on others, and determinations of right and wrong.

This synthesis requires, first, that we recognize and acknowledge the differences between these three alternatives, as well as the implications and consequences of pursuing one in isolation of the others. It requires, second, that we appreciate all three as simultaneously and consistently co-present. At the same time and in any given moment, in the same way and in every given situation, we identify ourselves, our perspectives on others, and our ethics.

This synthesis seems to require balance. Balance, however, does not reflect the kind of synthesis we would want. Although balance accounts for all the parts, it does not reflect consistency and simultaneity. Rather, it reflects comparison and contrast, more or less of one thing at any given time. Within balance is also a tendency to emphasize conflict and tension rather than accommodation and agreement. A better word is equilibrium because of its emphasis on maintaining the center. Equilibrium not only presumes balance, but also, according to the dictionary presumes, "equal balance between opposing forces." It refers to "that state of a material system in which the forces acting upon the system, or those of them which are taken into consideration are so arranged that their resultant at every point is zero." Equilibrium "returns to its original position after being disturbed."[1]

Another difficulty with balance is its tendency towards measurable differences. That attribute, as well as the implications and consequences ensuing from it, situates it solidly within the realm of the rational. Equilibrium represents the measurable, and also the immeasurable, the commensurable as well as the incommensurable to which Koestenbaum referred in his description of metaphor. It represents the emotional and the spiritual as well as the rational.

The difficulty with the kind of synthesis and equilibrium we are proposing is that its attainment is elusive and unattainable, allusive and impractical. We can never

---

[1] Edmund S. Weiner and John Simpson, eds., *Oxford English Dictionary* (Second Edition) On Compact Disc (Oxford: Oxford University Press, 1998).

achieve it. Nonetheless, it presents an ideal towards which we can strive, a dynamic towards which we can orient ourselves, our perspectives, and our actions. Its primary advantage is that it serves as a point of departure and return. It gives us something from which and towards which to assess those rare moments when everything seems to work together, and those frequent moments when something is missing, when something doesn't seem quite right. In those moments, we can ask whether we are sufficiently or insufficiently focused on ourselves and self-interest, on others and others-interest, or on the greater whole and its interests.

We are not proposing, then, a static proposition for self-identification, self-determination, or self-assessment, but a dynamic, never-ending process for all three. We are providing a basis for organizing our lives and our actions, a way of assessing our identities, our perspectives, and our determinations of right and wrong which accounts for all three, and which also leaves room for additional insights and discoveries within each. The ways in which we identify ourselves, our motivations and objectives, and our interpretations of right and wrong, become matters not only of synthesis and equilibrium, but also of dynamic process.

At the center of this complexity is opportunity; the opportunity to be the best we can be in every way, at any time, in any place. The driving motivation is to avail ourselves to opportunities: to become the best rational, emotional, *and* spiritual persons we can be; to be as independent, dependent, *and* interdependent as possible; to pursue wealth and distinction *and* surrender and compassion *and* transcendence and infinity. In all things, in every way, in all our actions, we want to be the best we can be. To do otherwise renders us and our values incomplete and inadequate.

Ignatius J. Reilly

Unfortunately, we have been shaped and formed to do otherwise. Ignatius J. Reilly has focused so intently and exclusively on himself that he can ask only one question: What can you do for me? Reilly, the fictional hero of John Kennedy Toole's novel, *A Confederacy of Dunces*, laments the "lack of theology and geometry" in today's world. He wears an old hunting cap with earflaps, baggy tweed trousers, a plaid flannel shirt, and a muffler around his neck. That outfit he considers "acceptable by any theological and geometrical standards, however abstruse, and suggest a rich inner life."[2] He alone has that "rich inner life."

"What can you do for me?" is translated into "Why can't you be like me?" At the center of attention, he wants others to identify themselves and to act as he does. He is so turned in on himself and his own closed, static perspective on life that he interprets the "possession of anything new or expensive" as reflective of "a person's lack of theology and geometry" and "could even cast doubts on one's soul." Distinguishing an "inner life" from an "outer life," he connects the two to one another, and assesses new and expensive clothing as "offending taste and decency" as violating a "natural order" grounded in comparisons and contrasts.[3] Clearly, he has subsumed the emotional and the spiritual into the rational, and relinquished any appreciation of transcendence and infinity or of surrender and compassion.

Ignatius would establish an internal and external continuity, but also a spiritual and rational continuity. He would agree with the artist Robert Lawlor's definition of geometry as "the study of spatial order through the measure and relationships of forms," and the intersection of theology and geometry, heaven and earth, the infinite and the finite, for "intellectual and spiritual insight."[4] As geometry is etymologically rooted in measurement ("measure of the earth"), so the spiritual would also be

---

[2] John Kennedy Toole, *A Confederacy of Dunces* (Baton Rouge: L.S.U. Press, 1980), 2.
[3] John Kennedy Toole, 153.

subjected to quantitative measurement. Accommodated to the rational, the spiritual would be subjected to rational mathematical principles.

As the story unfolds, we find that Ignatius is terribly lonely and isolated from others. His college friend Myrna writes to him from New York, and recommends "therapy of sex" because he has "closed [his] mind to both love and society."[5] He has not only failed to develop his emotional dimension, he has subsumed it into the rational. Others exist only as objects of his expectations, as failing to meet his expectations.

He can only pray for them. Even his prayer reflects absorption into self-interest. He prays for protection from his boss's demands, for respite from his gastrointestinal difficulties, and for release from his mother's intrusive behavior. In other words, he prays for what he can't or won't do for himself, and one thing he cannot do for himself is establish connections within himself, or with the experienced reality existing outside of himself. Even his prayer is directed to his own self-interest. He is asking of God and the saints: What can you do for me?

Many a loud prayer arose from my chaste pink lips, some of thanks, some of supplication. I prayed to Saint Mathurin, who is invoked for epilepsy and madness, to aid Mr. Clyde (Mathurin is, incidentally, the patron saint of clowns). For myself, I sent a humble greeting to Saint Medericus the Hermit, who is invoked against intestinal disorders... For my mother I sent a prayer flying to Saint Zita of Lucca, who spent her life as a house servant, and practiced many austerities, in the hope that she would aid my mother in fighting her alcoholism and nighttime roistering.[6]

Ignatius' mother is given neither to alcoholism nor to debauchery. She is enjoying her life, and consequently unavailable to attend to him or meet his every whim. Mr. Clyde is asking Ignatius to sell hotdogs, to make some money, rather than eating them all himself. "The grandeur of my physique, the complexity of my

---

[4] Robert Lawlor, *Sacred Geometry: Philosophy and Practice* (New York: Crossroad, 1982), 6.
[5] John Kennedy Toole, 69-70.
[6] John Kennedy Toole, 197.

worldview, the decency and taste implicit in my carriage," he writes in his journal, and "the grace with which I function in the mire of today's world— all of these at once confuse and astound Clyde."[7] They astound Mr. Clyde because Ignatius is eating his and Mr. Clyde's profits.

He wants his own independence, and translates it into a perspective which makes demands on others. He wants them to ascribe to his self-interest. He wants to be king. "What I want," Ignatius tells his mother, "is a good, strong monarchy with a tasteful and decent king who has some knowledge of theology and geometry and to cultivate a rich inner life."[8]

If not king, he would be a "mentor and guide," instructing others to adopt his same rational perspective on life, to learn from his "not inconsiderable knowledge of world history, economics, religion, and political strategy acting as a reservoir, as it were, from which these people can draw rules of operational procedure."[9] He would want others to learn as he did, and to proceed with life from his same appreciation of order and organization, of rational and physical principles. He would want to objectify everything and everyone for his own use, to direct them to his own self-interest.

The title of the novel is taken from a quotation from Jonathan Swift's "Thoughts on Various Subjects, Moral and Diverting" to suggest that "when a true genius appears in the world, you may know him by this sign, that the dunces are all in confederacy against him."[10] Ignatius, the genius, is in competition with everyone else, the dunces, who are in need of guidance and direction. Everyone exists in opposition to him, obstacles to the realization of his expectations, enemies who threaten him. At the very center of his identity is a focus on self-interest so fixed

---

[7] John Kennedy Toole, 195.
[8] John Kennedy Toole, 184.
[9] John Kennedy Toole, 232.
[10] John Kennedy Toole, reverse title page.

and so intent that others pale in comparison. In fact, they pale so much that they are all enemies, and his success and survival is contingent on his domination over them. Ignatius is engaged in a competitive battle for his own mastery, and designates everyone he meets, on whatever level of intimacy, as a dunce.

That repression of the emotional and the spiritual has had an impact on his ethics. Ignoring the emotional and the spiritual— or, more precisely, trying to interpret them with respect to the physical and the rational alone— has resulted in an inadequate assessment of right and wrong. Based exclusively in rational and physical principles, ethics has become little more than a set of rules, a code of conduct.

These rules and codes exist outside of, and apart from, ourselves as persons. As such, they function as regulatory agents imposing boundaries on our actions and reactions. That regulatory facility is grounded in measurement, as well as in a system of punishments which are also "measured to fit the crime." They neither refer to nor encompass the impulses of the heart and the soul. Rather, they would contain them and limit them, pursuing them only within the limitations imposed by the rational.

Moving from theory into practice, we know this to be true because most of our time and attention is concentrated on the rational. The emotional and the spiritual are relegated to the periphery. We attend to them only after we have met the expectations of the rational, and do so within the development and progression of our lives, as well as within any given day, week, month, or year.

Practically, we lose the full import of our own lives for ourselves and others. We value ourselves and others primarily in terms of our own usefulness to others and their usefulness to us. We value independence, achieved through wealth and distinction, and avoid dependence and interdependence.

Ignatius is such a refreshing, lovable character because he is so much like us.

111

He has not only been the willing recipient of the world's determining influences, with its inherent oppositions and contradictions, but also of the order and organization it has imposed on him. He has found that the easiest way to deal with it is to flow along in the progression of its current, striving for independence and its implied control of everyone and everything else. He has set himself up as the arbiter of good taste and appropriate behavior. He has also established himself as the exemplar of good judgment and good ethics, assessing right and wrong not only for himself, but for others as well.

Ignatius is not dumb. He has read and studied philosophy, theology, and mathematics. He has absorbed the American Dream, and has interpreted all of his learning as contributing to his own self-interest. Consequently, his perspective on others, on nature, and even on the divine, is guided by a closed, myopic self-identity. Never does it cross his mind that the divisions and qualifications, the contradictions and oppositions, of Greeley's second level of knowledge represent neither the totality of knowledge, nor the totality of his identity as a person, nor the totality of ethical determination of right and wrong. As we do so often, he has substituted a part for the whole, and then reinterpreted the whole to meet the requirements and expectations of that one part.

We, too, concentrate our attention on this second level of knowledge rather than on its original synthesis. That, we have learned to do because of the exaggerated focus on the rational in both formal and informal education. The question confronting us is that of doing otherwise. Can we assume an identity, a perspective, and a determination of right and wrong based in synthesis? Can we begin to think, feel, and act with respect to the opportunities afforded by a dynamic equilibrium?

We would, then, appreciate Ignatius as the antithesis of synthesis. His perspective is so dominated by his own independent self-interest that he cannot even begin to imagine other possibilities. He has no interest in adopting a perspective of dependence and others-interest or of interdependence and its interest in the whole. He cannot begin to imagine a synthesis which would incorporate the spiritual and the emotional as of equal value with the rational. He has neglected those opportunities afforded by his experience to attend to others and to God in terms other than his self-interests.

We, however, want all three. We want all three in synthesis, and want to value ourselves in terms of a synthesis of personal integration within our very identities, our perspectives on others, and our ethics. Before recognizing and acknowledging synthesis, we have to first recognize and acknowledge the driving and motivating momentum opposing it. With respect to the American Dream, we question why we are so driven towards wealth and distinction rather than towards surrender and compassion and transcendence and infinity.

Value and Perception

What we are really asking is how, and in what terms, do we value ourselves? Derived etymologically from the Latin *valere*, referring to worth and strength, value is defined first as "a fair return or equivalent in goods, services, or money for something exchanged" and second as "the monetary worth of something: marketable price."[11] Value refers to identity, perspective, and ethics, but with respect to numerical and economic comparison and contrast, for value is defined as "a

---

[11] Henry Bosley Woolf, ed., *Webster's New Collegiate Dictionary* (Springfield, MA: G.& CMerriam Company, 1973).

numerical quantity assigned or computed."[12]   It is not simply a matter of being treated as numbers, but of identifying ourselves as numbers. It is not a matter of having been assigned meaning in incremental measurements, but of ourselves assuming meaning in numerical terms. It is not a matter of our actions being judged by others in quantifiable comparisons and contrasts, but of assessing our own actions in those same terms.

We would value ourselves, other people and nature, and God in those terms, for, as the dictionary explains, value refers to "esteem, regard," but as an "estimate or opinion *of,* liking *for,* a person or thing" and "worth or worthiness (of persons) in respect of rank or personal qualities." It is also "the relative status of a thing, or the estimate in which it is held, according to its real or supposed worth, usefulness, or importance."[13] Even with respect to ourselves, and others immediately around us, we measure and quantify, compare and contrast, objectify and utilize.

We would also value the divine in terms of comparison and contrast, utility and objectification, measurement and quantification. Doing so, we would define God in rational terms, comparing and contrasting, quantifying and measuring degrees of difference. Doing so, we reduce God to rational objectives. Doing that, we value God in terms of her/his usefulness to meeting the objectives of our own self-interests.

But, is that really how we value ourselves? Is that what experience means? Is that what knowing ourselves, identifying ourselves, and judging our actions is really all about? Is personal identity simply a matter of attuning our bodies and minds, our hearts and our souls, to measurement and quantification, especially as these qualities have achieved the status of fixed and immutable law? Are our ethics simply a matter

---

[12] Henry Bosley Woolf, ed., *Webster's New Collegiate Dictionary.*
[13] Edmund S. Weiner and John Simpson, eds., *Oxford English Dictionary* (Second Edition) On Compact Disc (Oxford: Oxford University Press, 1998).

of governing our thoughts and actions according to laws of weight, motion, and resistance? That seems to be the case, for reason— with its principles and its conclusions— is the basis for assessing ourselves and our actions. That is the only conclusion we can reach when we focus not on knowledge itself, but on secondary reflection of that knowledge, especially when we limit that reflection to the quantifiable and measurable laws of nature.

With respect to Greeley's distinction, that is the only theoretical and practical conclusion we reach when we concentrate more on knowledge as defined by the "cognitive self" than as defined by the "agent intellect." If that is the case, it means that there is a difference between the two, and that we have lost something in moving from one to the other. It means that we define value numerically and monetarily. It also means that we have lost any appreciation of valuing ourselves, meaning, and ethics with respect to the synthesis inherent to metaphor, and to the "agent intellect."

Turning the tables around, however, and reverting to that appreciation of the metaphorical "agent intellect," we gain a very different appraisal of value, and of valuing ourselves. We find that our identities and our ethics are not simply quantifiable and measurable, or subject to universal and objective laws of nature. What we find is that we are also emotional and spiritual, and that we act and react in ways which do not correspond to measured laws of reason. We discover that their origins and causes, as well as their consequences and conclusions, cannot be encompassed or comprehended by universal and objective laws, whether governing perceptions or ethics. Actually, they challenge the validity of those laws, and do so precisely because they are unpredictable and spontaneous.

What would the mind and the body do with the heart and the soul? They would ignore them and dismiss them, judging them unreliable and unpredictable. They would subordinate and submerge them, rendering them secondary and inconsequential. They would subsume them into themselves, controlling and regulating them. They would do so to establish and perpetuate their own dominance and superiority. If the physical body and the rational mind establish the conditions for personal identity, then the emotional heart and the spiritual soul would have to be valued with respect to the laws governing the connections between the mind and the body. Failing to do so, they would be moved aside, relegated to the periphery, and assessed as accidental rather than essential. In short, if reality is attributed to the rational and the physical, it is not attributed to the emotional and the spiritual.

More obvious is the answer to the question, what would the heart and the soul do with the rational and the physical? Ignored and dismissed, subordinated and submerged, subsumed into the emotional and the spiritual, we would lose any sense of objectivity, regularity, and predictability; any sense of unique individuality and particularity, and any possibility of sizing ourselves up against others. So focused would we be on either connecting to other people and nature, or on interconnecting to the totality of the whole, we would lose any appreciation for ourselves as disconnected from others, as autonomous persons.

With respect to knowledge and experience as originally integrative and synthetic, we identify ourselves to be physical and rational and to be emotional and spiritual. There is something about us that can be prescribed, anticipated, projected, and expected. There is also something about us that defies categories, that cannot be contained in comparison or contrast, something that is unpredictable and spontaneous.

We would, then, appreciate knowledge and experience with respect to all four. At any given time, there is something about us that conforms to universal and objective laws of nature and reason, and something about us that doesn't. We know that there is something about us that can be measured and predicted, and something about us that can't.

The questions we've been asking recommend several alternatives for identifying ourselves and assessing our ethics. The first is perhaps the most obvious. We can focus on one or another of the dimensions of the total person— the physical, *or* the rational, *or* the emotional *or* the spiritual— and direct the whole of our lives to its realization and actualization. However, to direct all our time and attention towards one implies neglect of the others, and the lost opportunities of that neglect. We might also concentrate on one or the other aspect of experienced reality. There again, we are subjected to lost opportunities.

What do we have to gain to or lose in dividing ourselves in this way, in pursuing one basis for identifying ourselves and valuing our ethics according to the demands and concerns of one or the other? What we have to gain is a simplistic and inadequate appreciation of ourselves as persons. What we have to gain are divided identities, perspectives, and ethics, and an underlying need to switch gears in mid-stream, acting and reacting according to the situation and the moment.

Yet, we relegate our hearts and souls to the dictates of the rational, and we do so for control, for the security afforded by pursuing our own self-interests, and judging everyone and everything around us from that perspective. That impetus towards control has always been grounded in, and protected by, rational systems governing thought and action. Elaborate philosophical systems were constructed to sustain that order, and to organize society on the basis of the interplay between independence and dependence.

Consistent with these objectives, philosophy and politics joined hands, and society and its institutions were structured to establish and maintain control on the part of the independent, and obedience on the part of the dependent. To perpetuate this distinction, society and its institutions were structured hierarchically, with men and women organized along a continuum, and measured according to degrees of authority and obedience. That same hierarchical framework of reference, rationally defended within clearly defined castes, is now the domain of economics. Control over people and land is distributed with respect to wealth, with wealth and authority having become practically and theoretically synonymous.

In ethical terms, the great virtue is control, and as that control has become associated with wealth and distinction, those values have been associated with the pursuit of goodness. Because there is only so much wealth, and because it can be possessed by only so many, the pursuit of wealth has become individualized. So, too, has the pursuit of goodness. In contrast, dependence and interdependence are rationally assessed as absences.

That is, they really don't exist, or exist only when independence is absent. As independence is associated with goodness, dependence and interdependence are associated with evil, and both dependence and interdependence are relegated to the periphery of knowledge. Dependence and interdependence don't really exist because positive existence is attributed to independence. Evil is rooted not in wealth, but in the absence of wealth. That would mean that the values of surrender and compassion, and those of transcendence and infinity, would be avoided at any cost. If not interpreted as evil, they would certainly be interpreted as undesirable.

What we have done is redefined the very concepts of integration and synthesis to meet the principles and prescriptions of the rational. Self-knowledge, self-identity, and ethics are connected to one another, but according to rational prescription alone. How has that happened to us? Why has it happened? The answer lies, in part, with formal education, and its concentration on each of the parts of the whole as distinct, separated, and isolated from one another.

Perception and Identity

When we described the people and institutions forming and shaping us, we discussed the role of education as a major determining influence. Traditionally and historically, formal education influenced us in two ways. First, it focused on the individual as primarily rational. Second, it defined synthesis in terms of rational prescription. The implication is that, even when directing its attention to other people and nature, or perhaps to the divine, it did so with respect to the individual, and to the individual's self-identity as primarily rational. How often have we been told that we are "rational animals"?

Focusing on the individual, we also focus on self-interest, and on adopting a perspective which appreciates other people, nature, and the divine with respect to that self-interest. We assess everything existing outside of ourselves as either a contribution or obstacle, a friend or enemy. That distinction becomes the basis of self-worth, self-esteem, and self-valuation for assessing ours own identities and our perspectives on others.

We emphasize the rational, and enter into comparison and contrast, objectification and utility. We assess everyone or everything as having value only to the degree it contributes to our own self-interest. Doing so, we assess others as objects, and determine their value with respect to their usefulness to others. Useful, we keep them, perhaps even nurturing them. Useless, we discard them.

What has traditional philosophy taught us about ourselves, about our identities as persons? What has it taught us about knowledge, and about knowing ourselves? Basically, we learned from philosophy that the mind is everything, that we know ourselves rationally, and that we are human because we can think, conceptualize, distinguish, analyze, rationalize; because we can forge consistent and logical connections, draw logical conclusions, project universal principles and objective conclusions. Philosophy has also taught us that the mind is superior to the heart, the body, and the soul, and that any emotional, physical, and spiritual impulses and desires we may have need to be conformed to the mind and its facility for reason.

What we discover in the formal study of philosophy is an underlying focus on separation and distinction between subjects and objects. The individual person is a subject which grasps and perceives everything and everyone existing apart from it as an object. The conclusion, then, is that we are ourselves objects to others. The basis of connections and of relationships is defined with respect to differentiation, to comparison and contrast. These emphases are so pronounced that the connections and interconnections attributed to the emotional and the spiritual are relegated to secondary status. When they are discussed, they are reduced to principles of reason and logic. Also reduced or ignored are connections and interconnections.

So, too, are the values represented by dependence and interdependence relegated to secondary status. Attention is so directed to independence that we learn to focus on ourselves, and to value ourselves as compared and contrasted to others, as self-sustaining and autonomous. From that perspective we are led to value ourselves and others with respect to objectification and utility. Everything exists insofar as it is useful; everything is of value insofar as it is useful.

Inherent to philosophy is concentration on the second level of knowledge where we not only distinguish and separate, but also isolate and dislocate. Consequently we learn to focus attention on ourselves as isolated and detached individuals, and also learn to convert that isolation into control of other people and other things. Is the mind important? Yes, and so is its capacity for reason. In keeping with our appreciation for opportunity, we want to learn as much about ourselves as individuals as we possibly can. We want to be the best we can be as autonomous, self-contained individuals.

The psychologist and sociologist concentrate on differences and distinctions between ourselves and other persons, emphasizing the role of the emotions, and the identity of the person in relation to itself and to others, individually and collectively. Social scientists would answer questions of personal identity with respect to relationships with others, but would do so with respect to abstract definitions of society and of universal principles governing human relationships. Within that perspective, the emotions would be superior to the mind, body, and soul, and subject them to its own demands and expectations.

These relationships are ultimately reduced to rational propositions and principles, for society is defined as an object, as existing apart from ourselves, and in contrast to ourselves. We are to fit into it. Society has attributes of its own as distinguished from the attributes of the persons comprising it. Its point of origin is, however, the individual and individual self-interest. It is in our own best interests to accommodate ourselves to it. The emotions serve that self-interest, and are defined in a manner that invites comparison and contrast, objectification and utility. The surrender and compassion of dependence are, then, reduced to the boundaries and limitations of rational qualification and quantification, and ask: What can others do for me?

Yet, we want to be the best we can be emotionally, and appreciate the contributions of psychology and sociology in helping us to do so. But, we also want to be the best we can be spiritually as well. Theology has taught us not only that the soul is important, but that it is so important that it would dominate the mind, the body, and the heart. Even if we don't value the divine, or believe in the God of traditional Christianity, Judaism, or Islam, theology is important because it attunes us to the reality of "something other" than ourselves, the natural world, and the cosmic universe. It attunes us to the infinite, to the inherent transcendence and infinity of the mysterious dimension of life. However, even then it would define that attunement with respect to self-interest. Underlying its complexity of language and insight are the driving questions: What can God do for me? What can attunement to "something other" than myself, other people, nature, and the cosmos do for me?

The formal study of philosophy, sociology and psychology, and of theology and religion might assume the opposite perspective, that of dependence. We would, then, be led to answer another set of questions: What can I do for others, for nature? What can I do for society? What can I do for God? Rather than control, the great virtue becomes obedience to some authority outside of ourselves, whether directed towards another in particular, others in general, or some transcendent and infinite otherness itself.

The divergent poles of the rational and the emotional inform our identities, our perspectives, and our ethics. They also inform the manner in which we define knowledge and value for ourselves and others. They would have us divide ourselves, and choose to adopt either independence or dependence or interdependence as the single perspective from which to interpret reality, and from which to attach value to ourselves and others. On the level, of practical experience, they would direct us towards utility as the basic principle underlying our identities and our ethics which combine to reflect the manner in which we value ourselves.

That divergence becomes especially apparent in tension and conflict within each of the disciplines we are discussing. From a philosophical point of view, there exist two more-or-less-contradictory approaches, each with its own set of ethical imperatives. The deontological approach focuses upon foundational questions and accepts the end results that flow from a 'properly formulated' foundation. The teleological approach focuses upon benefits of the consequences of a given act.

Within each of these two broadly defined approaches, there exist yet finer distinctions. In the deontological camp, for example, there are monistic and pluralistic approaches. The monistic approach holds that there is but one principle from which the rules of conduct must flow. One well-known ethical theory of this type is Immanuel Kant's categorical imperative. It states that one should "act as if the maxim from which you act were to become through your will a universal law."[14] The pluralistic approach holds that there are a number of ethical axioms that need to be balanced in any given situation. W. D. Ross, for example, argues that there are seven *prima facie* obligations: promise keeping, reparation for harm done, gratitude, justice, beneficence, self-improvement, and non-maleficence. When conflicts occur between duties, we must intuitively decide how to balance these competing obligations.[15]

Teleological schema focus on maximizing the benefits to an individual or to society in general. Ethical egoism focuses on maximizing the benefits to an individual. Max Stirner claims that libertarianism stems from ethical egoism.[16] Two important exponents of utilitarian ethics are Jeremy Bentham and John Stuart Mill who focus on maximizing benefits to society.[17] The word *benefit* can have many meanings, depending upon who is using it. *Good* can mean happiness, pleasure, well being, or justice, or some combination of these qualities.

Common to both approaches, however, is the distinction between independence and dependence, and the question as to which perspective warrants attention and satisfaction. In both cases, the underlying emphasis is on value. Moreover, value is attributed to either self-interest or others-interest. In the final analysis, it is attributed to a mechanistic view of the person. The person is mechanized, and, as a machine, valued as useful or useless. So are the person's ethics.

---

[14] Immanuel Kant, *Fundamental Principles of the Metaphysics of Morals*, http://www.hkbu.edu.hk:80/~ppp/K1texts.html
[15] W. D. Ross, *The Right and the Good* (Oxford: Clarendon Press, 1938).
[16] Max Stirner, *The Ego and His Own* (New York: Benjamin R. Tucker, 1907).
[17] Jeremy Bentham, *An Introduction to the Principles of Morals and Legislation*, http://www.la.utexas.edu/labyrinth/ipml/index.html
John S. Mill, *Utilitarianism*, http://www.hedweb.com/philosoph/mill.

The business ethicist Joseph L. Badaracco cautions us against adhering to any of these "grand principles" of philosophical speculation for practical decision-making. Their objective, he claims was "extremely ambitious," but deficient. He claims that "philosophers sought to find an overarching, rational justification for morality— a set of basic principles that were independent of religion, tradition, culture, or individual beliefs." However, what they discovered was a "morality machine" which set the one fundamental ethical principle "at the end of a conveyor belt, and people could feed their ethical problems it. After a period of clanking and chugging, the machine would apply the fundamental principle to the problems and then give answers."[18]

Badaracco's message moves beyond business to life itself, reflecting the implications of exaggerating the rational to the neglect of the emotional and the spiritual for morality and ethics. Closed in on themselves, the ethical principles derived from philosophical speculation would have us close in on ourselves, and forget the emotional connections of our national and ethnic cultures and traditions and the spiritual interconnections of our religious beliefs. Philosophical speculation would support and encourage the American Dream and its appreciation of the person as an autonomous individual. Theology can do the same.

Questions of value arise with respect to relationships with God as well as with one another. Do we value God with respect to our own self-interests? Do we value God with respect to others-interests? Do we value ourselves with respect to God's interests? Early in the twentieth century, Rudolf Otto responded to these questions by claiming that religion encompasses both independence and dependence. In his classical study, *The Idea of the Holy*, he explains the opportunities gained and lost when interpreting our relationships with God rationally and emotionally.

He is assuming the existence of God, but not in traditional terms. His God is neither that identified through philosophical or theological speculation, nor that

---

[18] Joseph L. Badaracco, Jr., *Defining Moments: When Managers Must Choose Between Right and Right* (Boston: Harvard Business School Press, 1997), 35.

preached or worshipped in our churches, synagogues, or mosques. Neither is it the God contained and limited within the dogmatic statements and doctrinal propositions of any one religious tradition. Rather, for Otto, God represents that "something other than ourselves, other people, and nature" we mentioned earlier.

To underscore this point of view, Otto creates his own language. Rather than writing of God, he writes of "the infinite, transcendent numinous" and of the "wholly other."[19] The etymological derivation of the word numinous is the Latin verb *nuere*, meaning "to bow." This new language means that whatever God is, God is "other" than anything we know or experience, or anything or anyone else we encounter, meet, or perceive through our senses, or can be contained within either emotional or rational assumptions, so much so that it is "wholly other." Second, it means that the appropriate response and reaction of the person who has experienced the divine is one of humble submission, of nodding assent.

We are bowing because we are dependent. What are we really bowing to? From Otto's perspective we are bowing to God. Inherent to religious experience is an encounter with the infinite as simultaneously compelling and repelling, a *mysterium fascinans et tremendum*.[20] In Otto's language, the encounter with the *mysterium fascinans* moves the person beyond "love, mercy, pity, comfort" towards "bliss or beatitude," and even further towards a profound and overwhelming sense of "wonderfulness and rapture which lies in the beatific experience of deity."[21] On a more practical level, it translates into a perspective which we have been discussing with respect to the emotional. It focuses on dependence, and to connecting us with, and drawing us towards, other people, nature, the cosmos, and God.

There is, however, another dimension of the experience of the infinite which cannot be ignored, a second aspect of the encounter with the "wholly other." The

---

[19] Rudolf Otto, *The Idea of the Holy* (New York: Oxford University Press, 1958), 5-7.
[20] Rudolf Otto, 13, 31.

encounter with the *mysterium tremendum* moves from a sense of "'something uncanny,' 'eerie,' or 'weird'" towards "fear" or "dread," and even further towards "'shudder.'"[22] Practically, it turns inward; the person turns into oneself and away from everything and everyone else. It shrinks from relationships, as well as from any impetus towards being engaged or embraced by other persons, nature, the cosmos, or God.

Emphasizing either the dependence of the *mysterium fascinans* or the independence of the *mysterium tremendum* would direct us towards divergent perspectives and divergent ethical values. Either or both would, however, direct us towards valuing ourselves with respect to utility, to God being useful to us or to us being useful to God. Even combining the two, as Otto does, reflects an appeal to utility, and to valuing ourselves, other people, nature, and God with respect to utility.

Identity and Synthesis

To resolve this dilemma, we are tempted to turn to interdependence. That won't work. Interdependence, too, is often interpreted with respect to dependence and independence. We can easily construe attention to the greater whole, to God, or even to a principle claiming universal appeal with respect to utility. We can easily interpret our lives as surrendering to "something other than ourselves, others, and nature" or as using it to attain wealth or distinction. That, of course, is not true religion by any stretch of the imagination. However, we often find it described in those terms.

---

[21] Rudolf Otto, 31.
[22] Rudolf Otto, 13-14.

To describe "the structure of religious experience," the British philosopher John MacMurray contrasts reason and emotion with respect to science and art. Both focus on experience, but interpret it differently. For the scientist, value is derived from its utility, and "we are driven... to the conclusion that the attitude of mind which determines the selection and organization of the field of science is defined by a valuation of experience in terms of utility."[23] For the artist, it is a matter of intrinsic value, and "because the value that it has for me is intrinsic... my attitude toward it is contemplative and emotional, not analytic and intellectual."[24] Although not "analytical and intellectual," art can also appeal to self-interest, especially if that self-interest is directed towards surrender and compassion. Insofar as that is the case, it can also be useful.

Yet, there is something integrative about religion. Insofar as it brings the scientist and the artist together around a common theme, it reflects something of a synthesis. However, it would give priority to that point of commonality, and render both the emotional and the spiritual secondary at best, and negligible at worst. Moreover, that attempt at synthesis would recommend another form of objectification and utility.

It would also imply that spirituality is an antidote to the extremes of both the rational and the emotional. Rather than pitting them against one another, it could offer a false resolution to a real problem. We would not want to assume the rational and the emotional into the spiritual. Nor would we want to establish the spiritual as resolution to any and every difficulty we encounter. Rather, we would want the spiritual to stand on its own, as one part of a total synthesis.

MacMurray does, however, contribute to our discussion by proposing "intrinsic value," and by establishing an opposition between the "intrinsic value" of art and the

---

[23] John MacMurray, *The Structure of Religious Experience* (New Haven: Yale University Press, 1936), 10.
[24] John MacMurray, 11.

"utility value" of science. That first appreciation of value is diametrically opposed to that reflected in the dictionary's definition. Rather than attributing value to comparison and contrast, to numerical quantification and qualification, or to objectification and utility, "intrinsic value" attributes value and worth to the very fact of existence.

Intrinsic value, however, is not simply an attribute of art. It is also an attribute of experience of every kind, and as with economic opportunity costs, designates every dimension of experience as valuable in itself. Every person, every aspect of nature, and every expression of the divine has value of its own, by the very fact that it is experienced. We, then, attribute intrinsic value to independence, dependence, and independence; to the rational, the emotional, and the spiritual, and to the values represented by each.

As knowledge is integrative before divided, a whole before it is divided into parts, so is every aspect of experience. As we experience, so do we perceive, and our perspective is whole before it is divided. This means that we recognize and acknowledge differences among the three perspectives of independence, dependence, and interdependence, but unite them into a synthesis. Accordingly, this would mean that we value ourselves, and every and any thing outside of ourselves, as simultaneously independent, dependent, and interdependent. That value, in itself, extinguishes any motivation towards valuing anything in terms of objectification and utility. If every thing and every one has value, then we would not want to discard any aspect of our experience.

Recognizing how much our formal education has resulted in a greater appreciation for separation and division than for integration and synthesis, we can see how it corresponds to the American Dream. Emphasizing the rational, and appealing to the rational with respect to numerical comparison and contrast, we can see how it would direct us towards the pursuit of wealth and distinction as ends in themselves. Insofar as each area of learning, each discipline of formal education, would have us unite and integrate everything for its own interests, so, too, have we learned to do the same for ourselves. Moreover, we have learned to direct those self-interests towards a valuation of ourselves, and of everything and anything else, for its "utility value" rather than for its "intrinsic value."

For those reasons, Dr. Deborah DeZure, an education excellence specialist, recommends that formal education become more interdisciplinary, "pursuing knowledge that integrates and synthesizes the perspectives of several disciplines into a construction that is greater than the sum of its distinct disciplinary parts."[25] To underscore that recommendation, she provides six reasons:

> *First, there are pressing social problems (crime, poverty, AIDS) that cannot be resolved by a single disciplinary perspective. Second, students and faculty rail against the artificial fragmentation of knowledge, asking for more connected learning and coherence in the curriculum. Third, employers want college graduates who are prepared to meet the multidisciplinary needs of the work world, integrating what they have learned in disparate fields. Fourth, administrators hope to make more efficient use of resources and equipment by sharing them across disciplines. Fifth, there are dynamic changes in knowledge construction, blurring disciplinary boundaries across fields, e.g., cultural studies. And sixth, electronic technology and the Internet are transforming the way we organize and seek knowledge, replacing linear models with hypertext links that disregard disciplinary boundaries.*[26]

DeZure is opposed not only to what we have learned, but to what we have become as well. Is she right? To answer that question we need only begin counting the hours, days, weeks, months, and years that have been expended on formal education, and on rational thought. While we're at it, we might also count those expended on developing our emotional and spiritual dimensions. To realize the implications of that expenditure of time, we need only recognize the ease with which we're able to direct our minds towards realization of our objectives in almost any

---

[25] Deborah DeZure, "Interdisciplinary Teaching and Learning," *POD Network* (Athens, GA: Office of Instructional Development), Fall, 1998, 1.
[26] Deborah DeZure, 2.

situation or circumstance. However, when it comes to the heart and the soul, to relationships, we flounder in a sea of insecurity and uncertainty.

Implicit in DeZure's reorganization of education is a reorganization of the person, and a reinterpretation of identity, knowledge, and perspective. That reorganization would appeal to synthesis before division, and to an appreciation of the synthesis of the total person. It would also focus on "intrinsic value" rather than on "utility value."

All too often, we discuss or analyze our disconnections, our connections, and our interconnections by focusing on each isolated from the others. Internally, then, we direct attention to the mind, or to the heart, or to the body, or to the soul, and distinguish them from one another. Not only do we distinguish them from one another, we differentiate the objectives towards which each is directed, and the values which will lead us towards those objectives. Externally, we act and react with respect to the pursuit of wealth and distinction, or surrender and compassion, or transcendence and mystery.

The words we use to describe each of these dimensions and their objects can be easily modified; the meanings we attach to them qualified; the significance we attribute to them easily scrutinized. Yet, in doing so, we continue to focus on each as constituting a separate realm, as operative within a distinctive arena, and as fulfilling different functions at different times and in different situations. As they come to the fore, we find ourselves saying things like "Without health, we have nothing" or "God is number one in my life," or perhaps "all I really need is love." As we separate and distinguish each of these parts of the whole, so also do we separate and distinguish the values corresponding to each, and accordingly, valuations of right and wrong attributed to each.

On the level of identity and perspective, that synthesis is expressed clearly and boldly in Mark's Gospel, in Jesus' ethical imperative to love.

Listen, Israel, the Lord our God is the one, only Lord, and you must love the Lord your God with all your heart, with all your soul, and with all your mind and with all your strength. The second is this: You must love your neighbor as yourself.[27]

Basic to this answer is an appreciation of integrated synthesis. We are to love ourselves; we are to love others; we are to love God. The objects of love are not ranked in any kind of specific order of significance. One is not attributed with status over the others, nor is one rendered preferable to the others. We are to love ourselves, others, and God simultaneously and consistently. That is, we are to interpret and appreciate love of God, love of neighbor, and love of ourselves as arising from, and corresponding to a synthesis of perspective and a synthesis of expression.

That love represents the integrated synthesis of the total person, for it refers to the heart, soul, mind, and body not in distinction, but in unity. It also refers to the totality of experience, for it encompasses the infinite and the finite, other people and the divine, within an inherent dynamic of the whole. We would extend that dynamic to include nature and the cosmos, and to value the totality of the person as well as the totality of experience as encompassing and embracing a unified whole. It is a love corresponding to self-interest, others-interest, and the interests of the whole.

From this perspective, any tendency towards independence or dependence or interdependence exclusive of the others is simply inadequate. Also inadequate is any interpretation of love of God or love of neighbor based on individual self-interest alone. Also inappropriate is any interpretation based on the rational alone, or the emotional alone, or the spiritual alone. Also inappropriate is any interpretation of love of God and neighbor based on concern for others without an accompanying concern for oneself and for God. Also inappropriate is any interpretation which

---

[27] Henry Wansbrough, ed., "The Gospel According to Mark," 12, 28-31, *The New Jerusalem Bible* (Garden City: Doubleday & Company, 1985) 1678.

excludes anyone or anything, or would use anyone or anything for self-interest or others-interest.

This perspective on life in general, and on our lives in particular, need not be confined to a Christian perspective. It is also a Jewish perspective, for Jesus' words resonate with those of the *shema* in chapter six of the Book of Deuteronomy which proclaims that God is one, that we are to love God with our hearts, souls, minds, and bodies; that we are to embrace all of life, everything we think, say, and do from a perspective of integrated synthesis and interdependence. We are to clothe ourselves with love of God and neighbor, for ourselves and for others:

> *Let the words I enjoin on you today stay in your hearts. You shall tell them to your children, and keep on telling them, when you are sitting at home, when you are out and about, when you are lying down and when you are standing up; you must fasten them on your hand as a sign and on your forehead as a headband; you must write them on the doorposts of your house and on your gates.*[28]

There is no one or anything that can be excluded from this integrated synthesis of love of God, of neighbor, and of nature. There is nothing that can be valued with respect to our individual self-interests alone, whether directed towards dependence, independence, or interdependence; towards surrender and compassion, or wealth and distinction, or mystery and transcendence.

Anything less would reflect either ignorance of the opportunities presented to us in our experience, and failure to recognize and acknowledge them within our identities, our perspectives, and our ethics. We cannot love God without loving others and ourselves any more than we can love others without loving ourselves and God. Anything less is incomplete and inadequate.

---

[28] Henry Wansbrough, ed., "The Book of Deuteronomy," 6: 4-9, *The New Jerusalem Bible*, 232.

Why, then, would we reject this synthesis, and direct our ethics towards either our own self-interest, others-interest, or otherness-interest? We do so because we have been conditioned to focus our perspectives on ourselves, on others, or on God in different places and different times. Consequently, we assume different identities and different ethical standards in different situations, and find ourselves vacillating from one set of values to another.

Doing so, we lose anything approximating personal integrity and personal honesty. We lose our identities. That realization becomes especially apparent in our interpretations of life itself, as well as of our attitudes towards others, towards nature, and towards God.

Sources For
Chapter 4: Valuing

For the Definitions of "equilibrium" and "value"

Edmund S. Weiner and John Simpson, eds., *Oxford English Dictionary* (Second Edition) On Compact Disc (Oxford: Oxford University Press, 1998).

Henry Bosley Woolf, ed., *Webster's New Collegiate Dictionary* (Springfield, MA: G. & C Merriam Company, 1973).

For Ignatius J. Reilly

John Kennedy Toole, *A Confederacy of Dunces* (Baton Rouge: L.S.U. Press, 1980).

Robert Lawlor, *Sacred Geometry: Philosophy and Practice* (New York: Crossroad, 1982).

For the Discussion of Philosophy

Immanuel Kant, *Fundamental Principles of the Metaphysics of Morals*
http://www.hkbu.edu.hk:80/~ppp/K1texts.html.

W. D. Ross, *The Right and the Good* (Oxford: Clarendon Press, 1938).

M. Stirner, *The Ego and His Own* (New York: Benjamin R. Tucker, 1907).

J. Bentham, *An Introduction to the Principles of Morals and Legislation*,
http://www.la.utexas.edu/labyrinth/ipml/index.html.

John S. Mill, *Utilitarianism*, http://www.hedweb.com/philosoph/mill 1.htm, 1863).

Joseph L. Badaracco, Jr., *Defining Moments: When Managers Must Choose Between Right and Right* (Boston: Harvard Business School Press, 1997).

For the discussion of Religion

Rudolf Otto, *The Idea of the Holy* (New York: Oxford University Press, 1958).

For the Distinction of the Artist and the Scientist

John MacMurray, *The Structure of Religious Experience* (New Haven: Yale University Press, 1936).

For the Synthesis in Education

Deborah DeZure, "Interdisciplinary Teaching and Learning," *POD Network* (Athens, GA: Office of Instructional Development), Fall, 1998.

For the Gospel of Mark and the Book of Deuteronomy

Henry Wansbrough, ed., *The New Jerusalem Bible* (Garden City: Doubleday & Company, 1985).

135

5. Interpreting

Peter and Mary
Inspirational Reflections
Work and Family
Charting and Reinventing

We want synthesis, but we continue to interpret our lives with respect to the American Dream's dichotomy of independence or dependence: our identities with respect to the rational or the emotional; our values with respect to wealth and distinction or compassion and surrender. Virtually forgotten and practically ignored is any reference to the spiritual, to interdependence, or to transcendence and infinity. Without that dimension, we lose recognition and acknowledgment of a significant aspect of the synthesis to which we aspire.

That leaves us not only with a false synthesis, but also with inadequate identities, perspectives, and ethics. We cannot help but think and feel, rationally and emotionally, dissatisfaction and lack of fulfillment. As successful as we may be, as happy as we may be, there remains a yearning for something more. Immediately, we think we have to be more successful, or feel we have to be happier to satisfy that yearning. We need to work harder at one or the other, or both. Perhaps we're barking up the wrong tree. Perhaps we need another perspective for resolving that yearning. Perhaps we need something other than the rational and the emotional to direct our aspirations. Without the perspective of interdependence, we limit ourselves and lose the opportunities afforded by transcendence and infinity.

Even more, we need the equilibrium offered by synthesis from which to appreciate our many parts and the totality of our identities, our perspectives, and our ethics. Without a sense of, and sensibility to, integration and synthesis we experience ourselves as less than whole. As apparent as that realization may be in theory, we easily lose sight of it in practice.

That is because, in part, we do not recognize the need for that synthesis. It is also because, in part, we do not acknowledge its significance. It is also because, in part, the coercive and persuasive determining influences of people and organizations would direct us to ignore it, and lead us to focus our time and energy on the more immediate pressures and demands they impose on us. Turning our attention to three examples of those pressures divert our attention from synthesis, we will analyze scholarly interpretations of scripture, inspirational reflections on life, and practical advice on conflicts between work and family. Then, we'll take the insights and conclusions we have learned from these experiences and compile them into a chart for reorganizing our own lives.

Within this discussion, we'll introduce the virtues of obedience, cooperation, and commitment. As we have seen earlier, the American Dream's exaggerated emphasis on wealth and distinction reflects obedience to the determining power of people and organizations over us. Its secondary appeal to compassion and surrender enjoins us to cooperate with others and nature. Its neglect of transcendence and infinity signal the absence of commitment.

As we engage in the process of reinventing the American Dream, and our lives in America, we are beginning to see how easy it is to emphasize the rational, give some assent to the emotional, and neglect the spiritual. It is also easy to see why we do so, as so many others around us do the same even in proposing personal and inspirational models for identifying ourselves, assuming a perspective in life, and assessing our actions. As we'll see, they recommend that we focus on self-interest or others-interest while practically ignoring the interests of the "something other" and of the dynamic synthesis of the whole.

What we are questioning is how easy it is to lose the forest for the trees, to be so focused on one, or even two, aspects of our experience and knowledge that we ignore or avoid the synthesis of the whole.

Peter and Mary

The theologian Herbert W. Richardson examines the tension between dependence and independence within the Roman Catholic Church's theology. He also assesses the differences between the two as significant for an appreciation of personal identity and ethics. Basically, he describes a church "according to Peter," and a church "according to Mary."[1] He identifies these biblical images as representative of different organizational expectations within the church, and also within ourselves as members of the church. The question for Richardson is which of the two has precedence.

---

[1] Herbert W. Richardson, "Mother of the Church," *Current*, 5, 1965, 48-61. See also the summary of this article under the same title in *Theology Digest*, 14:1, Spring, 1966.

Acknowledging the original synthesis of metaphor, Richardson explains how easy it is for organizations and people to construct their own partial and inadequate syntheses. Richardson's use of the word "archetype," reflects metaphorical synthesis, for archetype "is a term which unites, or seeks to unite, a wide range of other terms which are quite distinct from one another, e.g., thought forms, patterns of behavior, institutional structures, rituals, etc."[2] He ties archetype to metaphor, suggesting that, for both, "we may not know precisely how [they] function, [but] we know that they function and have a peculiar kind of prescriptive power."[3]

That prescriptive power is realized in both organizational structure and organizational ethics, for "to the extent that terms participate in an archetype, they are shaped by it in some appropriate way."[4] The reduction of the original synthesis to the rational becomes apparent in the institutional church's identification, structure, and ethical expectations. It can also becomes apparent in the way its members organize their lives, and the way they have been led to order the many determining influences which have forged their identities and their ethics.

For Richardson, this means that our identities, perspectives, and ethics have been organized for us, and that we have assumed to ourselves the underlying expectations of the church's organization, identifying ourselves and our ethics in a manner that is "essentially external and impersonal... and legal."[5] That is, Christian identity and Christian ethics are defined with respect to the biblical image of Peter. That image represents the original synthesis of archetype, and grounds not only the church's structure and ethics, but also its rituals and its beliefs.

In Matthew's Gospel, Peter recognizes (or confesses) Jesus' divinity, and, in response, is told "you are Peter, and on this rock I will build my community."[6] It is

---

[2] Herbert Richardson, c. 48.
[3] Herbert Richardson, c. 48.
[4] Herbert Richardson, c. 50.
[5] Herbert Richardson, c. 53.
[6] Henry Wansbrough, "The Gospel of Matthew," 16:18, *The Jerusalem Bible* (Garden City, NY: Doubleday, 1985), 1636.

Peter who is given ultimate authority. It is Peter who is given the keys of the kingdom of heaven, and control over opening or closing the Pearly Gates to saints or sinners. It is Peter who decides who is good or evil, and what is good or evil.

The image of Peter assumed the proportions of archetype, and became the basic underling principle for organizing the church, and for organizing the lives of its men and women. That principle "rests upon a visible commission which has juridical and monarchical character."[7] For Richardson, an archetype connects the many different parts of the whole into an integrated synthesis, and directs that inclusive unity of the whole towards final, ultimate objectives.

However, as Richardson is suggesting, when that archetype is based on inadequate premises, its implications will also be inadequate. The Petrine archetype is inadequate because it reduces emotional dependence and spiritual interdependence to rational independence. Insofar as that is the case, its ethics are also inadequate.

Why would the church look at the whole of the Christian scriptures, focus on that one image, and then grant it precedence over any other? Clearly, the church has chosen to identify itself and its ethics with respect to rational independence to preserve its own interests, and has done so in a manner consistent with so many other organizations of our experience. It attributes its existence to independence and the exercise of its own authority, and would, accordingly, demand obedience.

It would do so with respect to the totality of the person and the totality of experienced reality. To be consistent, it would appreciate its identity, its perspective, and its ethics as representative of divine authority, and, by exercising its authority, demand obedience of its followers.

In other words, the primary role of the Christian man or woman is that of ultimate obedience to ultimate authority. Were we to first read Matthew's Gospel,

---

[7] Herbert Richardson, c. 48.

then turn to Luke's Gospel, we would interpret the great Marian hymn, the "Magnificat" as reflective of that ideal. This is clearly not the understanding of Mary that Richardson has in mind when he proposes his Marian archetype. It is, rather, an interpretation of Mary consistent with the Petrine archetype which would assume the voluntary surrender of the emotional dimension into the involuntary obedience of the rational dimension.

There is, then, as we saw earlier, a distinction between obedience and surrender. Although very much alike, and often used interchangeably, obedience is the expected response to the imposition of authority. Surrender, on the other hand, reflects voluntary giving of oneself in whole or part. In accordance with the Petrine archetype, Mary is obedient. Within the Marian archetype, she surrenders voluntarily.

Mary herself, as well as her prayer, is often interpreted with respect to the Petrine archetype. She is the obedient handmaiden of God, as we are to be obedient children of God:

> *My soul proclaims the greatness of the Lord*
> *And my spirit rejoices in God my Saviour;*
> *Because he has looked upon the humiliation of his servant.*
> *Yes, from now onwards all generations will call me blessed,*
> *For the almighty has done great things for me.*
> *Holy is his name,*
> *And his faithful love extends age after age to those who fear him.*
> *He has used the power of his arm,*
> *He has routed the arrogant of heart.*
> *He has pulled down the mighty from their thrones and raised high the lowly.*
> *He has filled the starving with good things, sent the rich away empty.*
> *He has come to the help of Israel his servant, mindful of his faithful love*
> *— according to the promise he made to our ancestors—*
> of his mercy to Abraham and to his descendents forever.[8]

---

[8] Henry Wansbrough, "The Gospel of Luke," 1:46b-55b, *The Jerusalem Bible*, 1688.

Mary, then, becomes a model for all Christians primarily because of her humble obedience to God. Those who are like her are good; they will be rewarded; they will be given positions of power; they will be filled with good things. Those who are unlike her are evil; they will be punished; they will be pulled down from their thrones; they will be sent away empty.

However, if read within the context of Luke's Gospel alone, and without prior reference or knowledge of Matthew's emphasis on Peter, we would discover a very different interpretation of Mary. In Luke's Gospel Mary represents another image or model of Christian living: the surrendering and compassionate person. It is that interpretation of the biblical image Richardson proposes as an alternative to the dominance of the image of Peter.

Rather than interpreting church identity, perspective, and ethics with respect to the image of Peter, Richardson proposes that the Marian image assume dominance. Rather than juridical and legalistic, the image of Mary would be "eminently personal and subjective... maternal... pedagogical."[9] The implication is that Mary, like Peter, enlists an authority, really a counter-authority, of her own which "consists in cooperating 'with maternal love' in 'the birth and education of the faithful.'"[10] This means that Mary represents the familial and nurturing "maternal authority" which takes the form of "love and care— Marian servanthood."[11] The rational image of Peter would be replaced by the emotional image of Mary.

Mary's prayer, the "Magnificat," would be interpreted with respect to voluntary surrender rather than with respect to imposed obedience. That is, Mary becomes the voice of loving and caring service, cooperating with other people, nature, the cosmos, and God to give birth to Jesus and his message for all people in all time.

---

[9] Herbert Richardson, c. 53.
[10] Herbert Richardson, c. 53. He is quoting Vatican II's "Doctrine on the Church," *De Ecclesia*, 63.
[11] Herbert Richardson, c. 54.

The Marian image elicits a more active surrender to Jesus than the passive obedience of the Petrine image.

For personal identification and personal ethics, Mary's "maternal authority" represents a more compassionate appreciation of the person, and the person's ethics, than does Peter's more juridical "legalistic authority." The Marian archetype "presupposes... weakness rather than sinfulness" because its authority is "substitutional and pedagogical," as Mary "rules [her children] only until the time when they are strong enough to rule themselves."[12]

The Petrine image commands a rational ethics of obedience to authority. The Marian image reflects an emotional ethics of cooperation among others. It differs from the image of Peter in that its final objective is personal dependence and others-interest rather than independence and self-interest. Emotional surrender is manifested in cooperation. The mature Christian, according to the Marian image, would cooperate with other persons, with nature, with the cosmos, and with God.

The image of Peter would, then, be reinterpreted to fit the Marian archetype. We would appreciate Peter as more emotional and less rational. When, in Luke's Gospel, Jesus tells Peter that "by the time the cock crows today you will have denied three times that you know me," he also advises him that "once you have recovered, you in your turn must strengthen your brothers."[13] That request seems to be directed towards surrender and compassion.

When, a little later in the Gospel, Peter actually does deny Jesus three times, his denial and recovery is attributed to human weakness rather than to sin. His response is more emotional than rational:

---

[12] Herbert Richardson, c. 55.
[13] Henry Wansbrough, "The Gospel of Luke," 22:32-34. *The Jerusalem Bible.*

At that instant, while he was still speaking, the cock crowed [a third time], and the Lord turned and looked straight at Peter, and Peter remembered the Lord's words when he said to him, 'Before the cock crows today, you will have disowned me three times.' And he went outside and wept bitterly.[14]

He wept because he had failed to cooperate; because he had failed to surrender. He did not weep because he had broken a prescriptive command or law. He had made a mistake, and through that experience, as we eventually discover, he became more attuned to the possibility of doubting, of questioning, of realizing that he possessed neither the complete certitude nor consummate assurance of rational control. When interpreted in terms of the Marian archetype, Peter is seen to represent emotional dependence rather than rational independence. The Petrine image is, then, subsumed into the expectations of the Marian image, with the latter assuming dominance for Christian identity and Christian ethics.

Richardson's insights and conclusions are interesting, and, to be sure, compelling. They are also consistent with the American Dream and its insistence on the inherent duality of the rational and the emotional for identity, independence and dependence for perspective, and the virtues of obedience and cooperation for ethics. But, is that all there is? Can we move beyond the two poles of this duality whether to interpret our lives in general, or even our lives as Christians?

To do so, we would want an image which also takes spiritual interdependence seriously. That is, Richardson's appreciation of the metaphorical archetype is flawed because it does not represent the totality of experience. In the same way, the American Dream is flawed. As a metaphor, it fails to account for the spiritual dimension of experience.

Rather than concentrating on the images of Peter and Mary as dominant metaphors, we need to grant that dominance to an even more comprehensive one.

---

[14] Henry Wansbrough, "The Gospel of Luke," 22: 60-62, *The Jerusalem Bible*.

We might propose, for example, that the love of God becomes the dominant archetype of the Christian life, and, as an image incorporate the spiritual as well as the rational and the emotional. Flowing from spiritual identity into an interdependent perspective, we would also move into recognition and acknowledgment of infinity and transcendence as significant values.

The addition of this third set of values would bring with it another dominant virtue. As the dominant virtue of the rational is obedience, and that of the emotional is cooperation, the infinity and transcendence of the spiritual would lead us towards commitment. Originally derived from the Latin verb *mittere*, meaning to send, and the preposition *com* or *cum*, meaning with, commitment denotes a continuing dynamic of "trust" and "an agreement or pledge to do something in the future." What do I agree to pledge or do in the future, or even now? Do I agree to obey as Peter, or to cooperate as Mary? Those are, of course, the wrong questions.

The right question would assume an appeal to commitment which would temper any tendency to exaggerate obedience or cooperation. We would ask, rather, does long-term commitment demand cooperation, obedience, or some accommodation to both? Introducing commitment into the mix brings into play the long-term and broad-ranged perspective of the future, even of the infinite. It demands that we look beyond the immediate when asking questions, and making moral decisions. It also demands that we look beyond any focus on our own self-interest or others-interest to bring that "something other" than ourselves and other people or nature into consideration.

Richardson is suggesting that the image of Mary's surrender and compassion is more representative of Christian living than the image of Peter's obedience to higher authority. He is perhaps responding to an exaggerated emphasis on the imposition of authority in much the same way that historians of New York City understood social reform as arising from the unbridled pursuit of wealth. He would swing the pendulum with full force into the opposite direction.

However, reading all of the scriptures, we cannot ignore the emphasis on obedience which appears throughout them. Neither, however, can we ignore the imposition of authority in so many areas of our lives. However, were we to appreciate it as only one dimension of our experience rather than the dominant dimension, we would assume a very different perspective. There do exist two other dimensions, two other perspectives, and they, too, would be recognized and appreciated.

Reading the whole of the scriptures we also find an emphasis on cooperation and an emphasis on commitment. We can interpret them to confirm either the perspective of independence, or of dependence, or of interdependence, and find justification for any of them. We can also interpret our lives from either of these perspectives, and justify doing so. But, do we want to justify the whole of our lives in terms of obedience alone, cooperation alone, or commitment alone? Wouldn't we have more to gain by availing ourselves to the pursuit of all three?

Sharpening our powers of observation and our skills of interpretation, whether for the scriptures or for our lives, we become ever more and more sensitive to the inclusive synthesis of the whole. We also become more and more aware of attempts to reduce that synthesis to the dominance of one of its parts. We also begin to recognize how easy it is to forget the whole, and to reduce it to the expectations of one of the parts.

Inspirational Reflections

We enjoy shopping for inspirational cards to send to friends and acquaintances on the occasions of birthdays or anniversaries, to mark significant moments in their lives or within the calendar year. We also enjoy reading them. We also appreciate the inspiration that originates in the lives of others, especially in written autobiographies or televised interviews, and in the lessons on life we draw from them. The synthesis we are proposing, however, enjoins us to take a careful look at those kinds of inspirational reflections, and to examine not only their conclusions, but also the implications of their conclusions.

In an interview with the American Indian activist and actor, Russell Means, he describes meeting an elder of the Lakota tribe near a pond:

> He said, "Pick up a rock. Throw it in the water." So I threw that rock in the water. He said, "That rock is your heart, and that first ring is your immediate family, the second is your extended family, and the third is your community. Fourth ring is your nation, fifth is your world. The next ring is the universe, and the outer ring is infinity." That's all he said. In an oral society you have to really listen. I saw that rock as my heart and what comes out from that heart affects infinity.[15]

Examining this story we can appreciate that the heart is metonymy for the total person. We can also appreciate how the heart is neither detached nor isolated, but connected to the whole of one's knowledge and experience, from the immediate to the infinite. The heart connects to people, close and far. It also connects to nature, the immediate and remote environment. It also connects to the divine, to transcendence and infinity. However, at that point, we would really want interconnection rather than connection.

As helpful as this metaphor is in describing the integrated synthesis of the total person connected to the integrated synthesis of experienced reality, it is misleading.

148

Its focus is on the individual, and on the individual standing at the edge of life. The heart moves out to other people, to nature, to the cosmos, and to the divine. There is connection, but what kind of connection?

For Means, the heart cannot be directed towards interdependence because it lacks any sense of integrated synthesis of the whole of experienced reality, and any sense of interactive connection to it. Lines are drawn, and people, nature, and God are separated from one another, categorized in contrast to one another. A chronological progression is implied, with an underlying message to concentrate first on the people immediately around us, then on nature, and then on God— but only if time and energy allow for those transitions.

His perspective offers two possibilities for identifying ourselves and our ethics. We can assume a perspective of independence, striving to identify ourselves and our ethics in terms of self-interest and an accompanying control of other people, nature, the cosmos, and God. We are responsible to ourselves and to the whole of experienced reality, but on our terms, in terms of our own self-interest. We might also assume a perspective of dependence, striving to identify ourselves and our ethics in terms of surrender to others, and acquiescence to others-interest. Responsibility would mean something very different, i.e., the ability to respond to the interests of others.

More often than not, we identify ourselves as vacillating between the two. Whichever seems to exercise the greatest pull or push at the immediate moment becomes most determinative our actions and reactions. Caught between the two, identifying ourselves and our ethics within that vacillation, we experience ourselves to be divided and separated, as two different people at different times and different moments, in different situations and different circumstances. Can we resolve that conflict and tension within ourselves? To do so, we would have to acknowledge the

---

[15] Catherine A. Wedlan, "A Regimen That Passes Means' Test," *Los Angeles Times*, August 10, S-6.

existence of the tension, recognize the conflict within ourselves, and seek some broader perspective by which and within which to situate our identities and our ethics.

That is, when we find ourselves in a dilemma, having to choose between good and evil, or even from an array of possibilities, we want a context for making those choices which will account for independence, dependence, and interdependence. Let us propose another diagram. That diagram would constitute a series of circles, with each circle representing the isolated autonomy and the intrinsic value of each aspect of the totality. Representing some degree of individuality and autonomy for each with respect to identity and perspective, other persons would be distinguished and separated from nature, from the cosmos, and from God, as well as from one another. However, while maintaining that individual distinction, we would also have those circles dynamically interlocking and interactively interconnecting with one another to reflect the original integrated synthesis of the whole.

Among those distinctions would be our own identities. Those individual identities would not, however, stand at the edge of the chart, or even at the center of it. Centralizing our roles, even within our own lives, would focus attention on ourselves, and appreciate everything and anything else as directed to and from ourselves, either for surrender or for control. Rather, we would situate our identities within the diagram itself, as one among many dynamically interconnecting and interlocking circles.

Rather than emphasizing the distinctive qualities of each, or of one aspect of the person to one aspect of experience, the focus would be directed first to integration and synthesis, and second to distinction and separation. Any tendency to assess the totality of experienced reality, or any part of it, in terms of independence or dependence would be assumed into interdependence. Any tendency to assess the totality of experienced reality, or any part of it, with respect to an ethics of power or an ethics of obedience would be assumed into an ethics of commitment. We would, then, be responsible for maintaining and sustaining that integration and synthesis.

Goodness and evil, then, become matters of sustaining or destroying that synthesis. Any exaggeration of one of the parts of the synthesis would represent evil, and the particulars associated with that exaggeration would be individual sins. Even then, identifying these individual sins is not an end in itself, but a means to the end. The end is identifying the one perspective, or the one dimension of our identities that is exaggerated. It is also a matter of identifying those we have ignored, or repressed, or avoided. We sin, then, by omission as well as by commission.

Given the fact that the integral unity of the synthesis is always being violated, we acknowledge, on a very deep level, that we are all sinners. Yet, attuned to opportunities of sustaining the synthesis, we are also virtuous when we direct our time, attention, and energy to them. Practically, we know this to be the case when we focus too much attention on ourselves, on other people, on nature, or even on God.

Turning to ethics, we are often urged towards responsibility for other people, for nature, even for the universal cosmos as a whole. We can, however, so easily interpret responsibility to meet the demands of either dependence or independence. With respect to nature, responsibility for ecological preservation could mean that we surrender to its course, and allow nature to evolve according to its own agenda rather than our own. We might also interpret responsibility for ecological preservation by determining how rivers and streams should be channeled, and how redwoods and owls should be protected from extinction.

To interpret values like responsibility or trust, or virtues like justice and mercy, we need first to clarify the basic perspective from which to pursue those interpretations. Basing our interpretations on independence results in very different consequences and implications than basing them on dependence. Were we to ground our interpretations in a synthesis of independence, dependence, and interdependence another set of consequences and implications would result.

From a more practical point of view, we can examine these differences with respect to basic underlying ethical values. A perspective focused on dependence, with its accompanying ethics of surrender, would motivate us towards wanting nature to take its course without any outside interference. We would allow for extinction of certain species of birds or animals. We would want to do everything we could to respect nature, and translate that respect into allowing it free reign to meet its own objectives.

A perspective focused on independence, with its ethics of power, would motivate us towards planning nature's course, and rationalizing that planning according to valid criteria and principles of preservation. We would study what precipitates extinction of certain species, and enact measures for preservation. A perspective focused on interdependence, and its ethics of commitment, would appeal to a broader consideration of its implications and consequences for nature, but also for people, for the cosmos, and for the divine. We would ask questions, perhaps a whole series of questions, pertaining to value, questions arising from a sensibility to transcendence and infinity. We would ask questions of intrinsic value, rather than questions of utility. We would survey all of the alternatives before making a decision.

We are proposing a fundamental change, a transformation or conversion, from the ways in which we have learned to identify ourselves and our ethics to new and different ways of appreciating ourselves, our motives— and to the translation of those motives into action and reaction. What we're trying to describe in this series of distinctions is the simultaneous presence of a threefold synthesis of perspectives. We are describing not only the ways in which the influences of our experience determine us, but the implications and consequences of pursuing either of these polarities in distinction from the other. Rather than suggesting that we choose one over the other, we are recommending awareness of that one thing, that one principle, which would acknowledge the polarity, but which would also surpass it.

We are recommending a synthesis reflected in opportunity— a synthesis of our identities, our perspectives, and our ethics with respect to the many opportunities afforded by all three. We are also recommending not only a consistency and simultaneity of synthesis, but also of reflection and action. What we are proposing is an appreciation of "consciousness" with respect to integration and synthesis.

Consciousness, as the dictionary tells us, refers to "awareness" and "awakening." [16] We awaken to ourselves through awareness of ourselves and others. Consciousness is, then, a matter of knowledge, for it is etymologically rooted in the Latin *conscire*, meaning "to know with." Knowledge, as defined by the same dictionary, is "the fact or condition of knowing something with familiarity gained through experience or association." [17] Knowledge arises from experience. From experience, we become conscious of ourselves; we know ourselves and identify ourselves. Conscious of ourselves, we act and react. Yet, the question remains as to what we're going "to know with" to identify ourselves.

We want to awaken to a synthesis of ourselves as persons and to a synthesis of perspectives and identities. We want to reflect that synthesis in our actions, and in our assessments of good and evil. The word "conscience" is also etymologically derived from the Latin *conscire*. As such, it represents an intimate connection of knowledge, identity, and determination of right and wrong action. A second question arises: What are we going "to know with" to distinguish right and wrong?

---

[16] Henry Bosley Woolf, ed., *Webster's New Collegiate Dictionary* (Springfield: G.&C.Merriam Company, 1981).

What the common etymological origin of consciousness and conscience reflects is continuity between the two. Continuity implies a consistency and simultaneity between personal knowledge and personal ethics, and appreciates the two interacting in the same way at the same time. A third question arises: What are we going "to know with" for continuity between identity and ethics?

What our actions reveal about ourselves is that we are neither exclusively dependent nor independent, but also interdependent. Ethical assessment reveals that we distinguish right from wrong with respect to all of our values. Obedience, cooperation, and commitment on the level of ethical assessment, or conscience, represents continuity with independence, dependence, and interdependence on the level of perspective. It also represents continuity with the rational, the emotional, and the spiritual on the level of identity.

That continuity, in turn, represents consistency and simultaneity of thought, speech, and action— of thinking, speaking, and acting in the same way and at the same time. The integrated synthesis of the total person, along with that of the totality of experienced reality, moves from consciousness to conscience, and from conscience to consciousness. There is, then, a dynamic simultaneity and consistency of thought and action connecting the integrated synthesis of the total person to the integrated synthesis of the totality of experienced reality, with that connection itself grounded in an integrated synthesis of thought, speech, and action.

When we concentrate on the interplay between dependence and independence, and lose sight of interdependence, we lose that perspective of the whole. It disintegrates into an emphasis on independence or an emphasis on dependence. It also assumes chronological progression, suggesting that what is good for us at one time in our lives is not good at another. To better understand the implications and

---

[17] Henry Bosley Woolf, ed., *Webster's New Collegiate Dictionary.*

consequences of pursuing dependence or independence, let us see how Dr. Laura Schlessinger "rationalizes" the absence of interdependence in her own life.

Work and Family

When Dr. Laura, the popular radio talk-show host, assesses her life, she does so with respect to independence and dependence. She describes her life as having two parts. "For years," she explains, "my whole life was my career— as a scientist, writer, teacher, therapist, and radio host. I believed that my well-being and feelings of success would come from my work." Then, "at 35, I discovered I was wrong, fell in love with my husband, Lew, and learned to be a mother." [18]

For Dr. Schlessinger, pursuing a successful career or a happy family is a matter of right and wrong. Also a matter of right and wrong is a parallel contrast between having once invested in "the material world" and now investing in "spiritual and emotional health." They contradict one another. That contradiction is contained within a dual perspective which assumes a need to emphasize either dependence or independence. Also a matter of right and wrong is work and family, with the former described with respect to self-interest and the latter with respect to others-interest:

> *When work takes away from our family, it serves only to expand and gratify our egos. We may see our family as the enemy— demanding more of what "we already gave at the office"! Just the thought of talking with our spouse or playing with the kids takes too much energy, we think. So we avoid going home, believing we have the right to some solitude and replenishment. But family is the replenishment. When we sever connections with family, friends, and God, our lives lose meaning.* [19]

[18] Laura Schlessinger, "What Is A Well-Lived Life?" *Parade Magazine*, March 15, 1996, 4.
[19] Laura Schlessinger, 4.

In these few words, she has unearthed several of the implications and consequences underlying our discussion. She is claiming that it is wrong to pursue independence and right to pursue dependence and that it is wrong to pursue self-interest and right to pursue others-interest. She extends that distinction to categorize work and individual autonomy with respect to independence, and family and relational connections with respect to dependence.

To explain her position, she writes that one has to recognize the polarities, and that one has to choose dependence and others-interest over independence and self-interest:

> *Frankly, I don't believe in balance. I know it's a hot topic. In fact it's this decade's Holy Grail. Not only do we want it all, but we also want it perfectly balanced. That's a fantasy, but desperately pursuing it lets us avoid making difficult choices.*[20]

She has made a fundamental choice. Choosing to pursue dependence and others-interest, she has foregone the opportunities afforded by independence and self-interest:

> *I've often been told I could make a lot more money if I would make more public appearances, travel more. But then I'd get to spend a lot less time with my family, and there just isn't enough money in the universe to make that appealing.*[21]

We would have to agree with her, but only if we, too, were identifying ourselves and our ethics primarily with respect to independence or dependence. We would also have to agree that the choice of one involves the lost opportunities of the one rejected. We would also have to agree that any appeal to balance provides an inadequate basis from which to assess our identities, our perspectives, and our ethics.

However, were we also to identify our perspectives with respect to synthesis, and our ethics with respect to commitment, as well as obedience and cooperation, we would have to disagree with her. Synthesis would not assess work and family as contradictory. Nor would it force a distinction between self-interest and others-

---

[20] Laura Schlessinger, 4.
[21] Laura Schlessinger, 4.

interest so decisive that it would require rejection of one for pursuit of the other. Rather, synthesis would establish a connection between the two on both the level of self-identity and the level of ethical decision-making. It would require that we become aware, that we awaken, to that one thing about ourselves which is common to both family and work. That one thing is the impetus to concentrate on the integrated synthesis of the whole before the distinction and division of its parts.

Can we have it all? Yes, but not to the same degree at any given moment or in any given time. Opportunity-cost decision-making assumes that the more emphasis we place on one thing, the less emphasis we'll place on others. For an appreciation of synthesis, right and wrong isn't a matter of absolute acceptance and absolute negation of one thing or another. Ethical decision-making is not a matter of balance, but of equilibrium. The dynamic process towards equilibrium becomes a primary concern, and tempers any tendency towards the extremes.

When we become too immersed in self-interest, a bell rings, an alarm goes off, to redirect us towards others-interest and to the interests of that "something other" than ourselves and others. Relating to others, to nature, to the cosmos, to the divine, that same alarm would return us to an appreciation of otherness and of intrinsic value when too focused on objectification and utility. As soon as we're pursing any matter or concern from an emphasis on its usefulness to us, the ethics of commitment would remind us to stop, look, and listen to other impulses of our experience.

Why is Dr. Schlessinger so adamant about choosing dependence over independence? The answer to that question lies, in part, within her experience, and the absence of the spiritual in her early life. Only later does she realize what she missed:

Growing up, I had no religious teaching and didn't realize what I was missing. I was smart and intellectual pursuits satisfied me. But the experience of becoming a mother created in me a desire to discover a context for the new and very deep feelings I had for my son. In my study of religion, I discovered a deep kinship with Judaism, the religion of my father, and all of us have now converted.[22]

To appeal to an old cliché, we might ascribe her enthusiasm for religion to the zeal arising from her recent discovery and conversion. We might also ascribe it to failing to recognize and acknowledge dependence and surrender in the early part of her life. Had she focused on others, on nature, and on God, as well as on herself throughout her life, she might have a different appreciation of herself, her identity as a person, her perspective on everything existing outside of herself, and on her ethics.

Her conversion is not uncommon or unusual. It is the expected response of the person who has focused so intently for so long on self-interest, and on the pursuit of the wealth and distinction of the American Dream. There comes a breaking point. We assess ourselves. We've pursued the American Dream. We've achieved success and distinction. We've done everything we were supposed to do? We question ourselves. Why, then, am I not happy? Why do I feel dissatisfied and unfulfilled? What's missing in my life?

We turn to the immediate, quick fix, and to an appreciation of our connections with others. We think that the inadequacy and emptiness we experience is directly related to failing to focus on other people or on nature because we haven't stopped "to smell the roses." Having achieved success, we want to be happy, and turn our attention to others. We begin to realize what we've been missing, how surrender and compassion result in happiness.

After pursuing dependence rather than independence for awhile, a light

---

[22] Laura Schlessinger, 5.

bulb goes off one day. We've experienced success and we've begun to experience happiness. Still, something is missing. We begin to confront morality and death. We ask questions about ourselves, our value as persons, our contributions to the world around us. Seeking answers to those questions, and wanting to fill the gaps we experience, we turn to religion, to God, to that "something other" that exists besides ourselves and the people and nature of our immediate experience. We begin to draw interconnections, and realize the possibilities for attaining bliss.

Why wait for that to happen? Why not pursue all three now? Dr. Schlessinger waited, and where has it led her? Apparently, she is pursuing happiness, but can't seem to distinguish happiness from bliss, so she equates the emotional and the spiritual, and focuses on love for her family as somehow reflective of both. She has equated love for her husband and her child with love of God, and in doing so has collapsed God into her family. God is no longer "something other" than her family. She has gained happiness, but has lost any opportunity for bliss. She has failed to see the opportunities afforded by relating to God as God.

What her experience is revealing to us is the inadequacy of failing to attend to the integrated synthesis of the total person at any and every moment of our lives. What is wrong, for her and for everyone else, is not her devoting time to her career rather than to her family. What is wrong is ignoring or repressing the emotional and the spiritual to pursue the rational, or ignoring or repressing the rational to pursue the emotional or the spiritual.

We are charting a new course for a new life, if not for others, at least for ourselves. It is a course built not of simple acquiescence to the determining influences we have been given. It is a course built on converting those influences into an integrated synthesis for self-knowledge and self-identity, for consistency and simultaneity between the two, and for assessing our actions and reactions.

Is that kind of conversion possible? It is, if we're willing to swim against the tide, and assume responsibility for the whole of our experience, knowledge, identity, perspective, and ethical decision-making. That kind of change, of transition, of transformation is possible only if the integrated synthesis of the whole becomes for us more important than any one of its parts. For that to happen, we'll have to change some of our assumptions, like that of the primacy of work in the lives of men, and primacy of family in the lives of women.

That change is already taking place. Women, as well as men, are working. However, raising children continues to be primarily a responsibility of women rather than of men. It is women who have to balance work and family. Arlie Russell Hochschild, wants a "more family-friendly workplace" to accommodate women with children.[23]

She wants more "flex time, job sharing, maternity and paternity leave, or part-time work" because companies have corporate cultures that reward "workers more for the time they put in than for what they accomplish."[24] She is assuming that both men and women work, and that work dominates their lives and everything about their lives. Wanting companies to accommodate women with children, she presumes that both men and women will prioritize their lives with respect to the demands of work.

In other words, we are so obedient to those determining influences which would have us assume that our lives— and our identities and values— will be dominated by work, we don't really question whether that is necessarily the case or

---

[23] Arlie Russell Hochschild, "A Work Issue That Won't Go Away," *New York Times*, Monday, September 7, 1998, A17.

whether we have any alternatives. Leah Hager Cohen argues that we do have alternatives: women can reject or escape this determination by asserting their independence, by refusing to juggle work and children, by choosing to direct attention to children rather than to work. "Through the work of caring for children," she confesses, she finds herself "stretched and exposed, distracted and dazzled," and that she is "learning to love the mishmash, boldly and unapologetically."[25]

She seems to be assuming that the rational order and organization of the workplace is more appealing and more satisfying than the emotional spontaneity and capriciousness of the home. She also seems to be assuming that the former is preferable to the latter. What she is really assuming is the overpowering and exaggerated preference for the rational the American Dream would have us pursue.

She describes her sister's experience in a manner suggesting similarities to her own, and recommends a preference for the emotional values inherent to parenting as opposed to the rational values inherent in work.

> It wasn't that she couldn't handle working the long hours at the office as well as at home, or making the twice-daily transition between roles. What she found intolerable was the feeling that she was constantly shortchanging both her work and her family. It was the parceling out of her energy, and the skimping compromises this forced, that eventually drove her to quit her job.[26]

What these women are really describing are the difficulties of acting and reacting within stereotypes of the respective roles of men and women, but also of the need to choose dependence or independence. They are so focused on traditional roles and traditional ways of identifying themselves, that they cannot change either. They cannot begin to envision another perspective on life which differs radically from that

---

[24] Arlie Russell Hochschild, A17.
[25] Leah Hager Cohen, "Joy. Frustration. Motherhood," *New York Times*, *Monday, September 7, 1998*, *A17.*

they were influenced to expect, shaped to assume. They cannot embrace the integrated synthesis of the total person— the rational as well as the emotional, and the spiritual— and to base their choices on an appreciation of the dynamic synthesis of the whole.

Distinguishing work from parenting, and the rational from the emotional, they are implying that we have to choose one over the other, that one is better than the other. The integrated synthesis, with its appeal to equilibrium rather than balance, would venture beyond that kind of choice, as well as the gains and losses of emphasizing one set of opportunities over another. The real choice presented to us is that of pursuing integration and synthesis, or that of choosing the conflict and tension between independence and dependence. Before making that choice, however, we first need to recognize the havoc wrecked upon us by the determining influences of the people and institutions of our experience.

The first step in that process is awareness and acknowledgment of the many forces and pressures that have been imposed on us, that have defined us, that have programmed us, that have determined us to be nothing more than a collage or composite of their influences on us. We have to *name* those influences. Second, we need to *claim* them as our own. We also need to name and claim the degree to which they have influenced us, some more than others, some more directly and more definitively than others.

We have to face them head on, and acknowledge just how much they have already influenced and determined our identities, negotiated and directed our actions, assessed and guided our ethics. We cannot, then, deny, neglect, repress, or ignore them, especially with respect to self-knowledge and self-identity. Third, we need to *tame* them. That is, we need to filter them through ourselves, interpret them for ourselves.

---

[26] Leah Hager Cohen, A17.

To do so, we can take the easy way out. We can filter and interpret our identities and our ethics through the lenses that have been given to us. We can respond and react to the power of the determining influences imposed on us by adopting them for ourselves. We can interpret all of life according to a principle of dependence with its accompanying values of surrender and compassion. We can rebel against that determination, and pursue life through the lenses of independence with its accompanying values of distinction and wealth. Both of those responses are expected. We've been disposed and programmed towards one or the other.

A third possibility presents itself. We can overcome these determining influences, and their determination towards either dependence or independence. We can unite and connect them, surmount and surpass them. To do that, we would neither annihilate nor obliterate them. What we would destroy is the assumption that these are the only two categories sufficient for ordering and organizing our lives. Actually, recognizing their deficiencies, especially in their implications for ethics and their consequences for action, we would want something else on which to base our identities as persons, and the ethical determinants of right and wrong flowing from them.

Charting and Reinveting

That acknowledgment and appreciation can be pursued only by examining our own human experiences and personal histories. That is, rather than charting personal self-knowledge and personal identity towards a projected, abstract ideal, we begin with ourselves, here and now, as we experience ourselves within this world, within this moment in time and place. The first questions we ask are: How did I get here? How did I become who I am? The answer to that question relies on identification and assessment of past experience, on naming and claiming the determining influences of others on personal identity.

It is also a matter of organizing those experiences for ourselves, for synthesis at this point in our lives. It is also a matter of taming them. We want to assess ourselves, our emphases, and the gained and lost opportunities we have encountered. Third, we want to address the future, and to project a plan or a chart for reorganizing ourselves towards future realities and possibilities.

We become aware, appreciate, recognize and acknowledge all of the implications and consequences of the synthesis we have been describing:

Its accounting of the whole of experience, of the personal and institutional influences that have, and continue to, shape, form, and define us. We would want to be sensitive to every aspect of our experience, and how it has contributed to our knowledge and to our identities. Nothing would be left out, not even those experiences which seem to be fleeting and inconsequential, as so many of those pertaining to interdependence. We would want, especially, to question what impact they have on us, and how they have affected us.

Its dynamic presence within knowledge, identity, and perspective and ethics. In other words, we would not only want to account for the physical, emotional, spiritual, and rational dimensions of the person, but also account for all of them as consistently and simultaneously co-present. We would attribute that same consistency and simultaneity to independence, dependence, and interdependence, as well as to the values respectively attached to each: wealth and distinction, surrender and compassion, transcendence and mystery.

Its uniqueness. It is unique and personal, because no one has experienced the same determinative influences in the same way and to the same degree of intensity. It is also unique and personal because no one achieves synthesis of mind, heart, body, and soul in the same way. It is a project because it is never ending. As soon as a new experience, especially one powerful and influential, enters into the person, the synthesis becomes nuanced and shaded.

Its direction and motivation towards ultimate meaning and significance. There is nothing short-term or immediate about it. It would provide a broad, long-term perspective even for immediate goals and objectives. It would answer the questions: What is really important to me? What do I really want out of life? What do I do to get there?

Its gained or lost opportunities. Assessing our actions and reactions, we would do so with respect to gains and losses, to advantages and disadvantages, to whether they contribute to or deflect us from achieving synthesis.

What will do that for us? What will meet all of these criteria? Immediately, we would want to identify that one principle with respect to what has already been given to us. *Family*, some would suggest. *Work*, others may recommend. Perhaps we might want to identify that principle with respect to more lofty ideals we have been taught, like *Happiness, Success*, or *Bliss;* perhaps *Love of others, Love of God*, or *Love of Learning*. We might even want to identity it in terms of less lofty goals, perhaps with respect to *Wealth* or *Money*, or the accumulation of *Material Possessions* or *Financial Security*. We might even think long-term, and direct our efforts towards the *Ease of Retirement* or to what we would want to look back to as our unique *Contributions to Life at the Time of Death*.

The dynamics inherent to opportunity costs would caution us with respect to any of these as valid and adequate for establishing and maintaining the integrated synthesis we are pursuing. Pursuing either of these would necessarily involve the lost opportunities of pursuing any other. To choose one would involve the rejection of others, as well as the emotional, rational, and spiritual costs of that rejection. The dynamics of assessing our many opportunities would also caution us with respect to directing attention to any one perspective, whether towards self-interest, others-interests, or the interests we associate with the divine. To emphasize either of these alternatives would necessarily involve rejection or negation of the others.

Although proposed by Joseph Campbell with respect to bliss, we might call to mind his analogy of the wheel of fortune, and the implication that we have more to gain from focusing our attention on the hub of the wheel rather than on any of the spokes along the rim. However we identify that hub for ourselves will determine not only how we pursue life, but also how we pursue success, happiness, and bliss. Perhaps the question is not what will provide all three, but what will avail us to all three, and open the doors for the many opportunities to be the best we can be.

Sources For

Chapter 5: Interpreting

For Definitions of "consciousness," "knowledge," and "conscience"

Henry Bosley Woolf, ed., *Webster's New Collegiate Dictionary* (Springfield: G. & C. Merriam Company, 1981).

For the Discussion of Scriptural Interpretation

Herbert W. Richardson, "Mother of the Church," *Current*, 5, 1965. See also the summary of this article under the same title in *Theology Digest*, 14:1, Spring, 1966.

Henry Wansbrough, "The Gospel of Matthew," *The Jerusalem Bible* (Garden City, NY: Doubleday, 1985).

Henry Wansbrough, "The Gospel of Luke," *The Jerusalem Bible*.

For the Discussion of Russell Means' Analogy

Catherine A. Wedlan, "A Regimen That Passes Means' Test," *Los Angeles Times*, August 10.

For the Discussion of Work and Family

Laura Schlessinger, "What Is A Well-Lived Life?" *Parade Magazine*, March 15, 1996.

Arlie Russell Hochschild, "A Work Issue That Won't Go Away," *New York Times*, Monday, September 7, 1998.

Leah Hager Cohen, "Joy. Frustration. Motherhood," *New York Times*, Monday, September 7, 1998.

6. Reinterpreting

Organizing Ourselves
Organizing Business
Moving Ahead

The American Dream would control us, and everything about us. It would exercise that control through an oppressive imposition of power from which we would respond and react by assuming that same power to ourselves. To do so, we are presented with several alternatives, several paths to pursue.

The implication is that we have some choice, some freedom from which to select one or more of these alternatives. Perhaps the selection has already been made, but we're unaware of it. Perhaps we're ready to break the chains that have bound us, and are now ready to change course. In the final analysis, though, that choice is expressed in our actions, especially in the manner we relate to other people, to nature, and to God. It is on this level that we really identify ourselves and our perspectives on life, and reflect clearly and loudly, for everyone to see and hear, what we're really about and what is really important to us.

169

In short, everything we do says something about us, reveals what is really important to us, reflects our identities, our perspectives, and our ethics. So we assess our actions, and ask whether we are primarily greedy and selfish, caring and sacrificing, yearning and aspiring. What do we find there? In our actions? We find that we are all three, but that, at any given time, one of these sets of alternatives seems to dominate. We look even deeper, and question which is really underlying even those moments, and actually setting direction for the whole of our lives. Which is really active and alive within and without us? Which provides the springboard from which we assess our relationships with ourselves, with others, with nature, and with the divine?

In Luke's Gospel, Jesus tells the story of the Pharisee and the tax collector who one day went up to the temple to pray.[1] The Pharisee prayed:

> *I thank you, God, that I am not grasping, unjust, adulterous like everyone else, and particularly that I am not like this tax collector here. I fast twice a week; I pay tithes on all I get.*

The tax collector "stood at some distance away, not daring even to raise his eyes to heaven; but he beat his breast and said,"

> *God, be merciful to me, a sinner*

Assessing our relationships, we assess ourselves, with respect to others, to nature, and to that "something other" than people and nature. As we do so, we cannot help but judge ourselves as falling short of meeting all of our own expectations or those others impose on us. Yet we strive to do so, patting ourselves on the back when we succeed, and begging forgiveness when we fail.

The great sin, then, is that of self-righteousness, focusing so intently on our own self-interests that we identify the interests of others, of nature, or of God in terms of

---

[1] Henry Wansbrough, ed., "The Gospel of Luke," 18:9-13, *The New Jerusalem Bible* (Garden City, NY: Doubleday & Company, 1985), 1719-1720.

our own self-interests. That is the sin of the Pharisee. Not all Pharisees are like this one. For the people of that time and place, Pharisees are revered and esteemed, respected and honored because of their relationships with God. Jesus' story is effective because it is disturbing. This particular Pharisee's prayers and actions betray discontinuity between what he claims to be about and what he is actually about.

We find the same discontinuity with the tax collector. In his time and place, the tax collector is despised and disdained. He is collecting taxes for the Romans who are occupying Judea and Gaililee and depriving its citizens of their own ethnic, religious, and political sovereignty. Yet, he knows himself to be yearning and aspiring for God. Rather than focusing on himself as does the Pharisee, he is focusing on God, but to the neglect of others. Not only is he neglecting others but he is also contributing to their oppression.

Not all tax collectors are like this one, and to assume that either this Pharisee or this tax collector is representative of all Pharisees and tax collectors would lend itself to the kind of stereotyping against which we are arguing. It would also lead us away from assessing ourselves, and our own identities and ethics, by focusing on others and judging others. In other words, it would lead to the very kinds of attitudes and actions we attribute to self-righteousness.

The underlying message of the story is that there is something of the Pharisee and of the tax collector within each and every one of us. There is something about us that is self-righteous, and it is only when it is carried to the extreme that it is sinful. There is also something about us that is righteous with respect to God. But to focus so intently on the spiritual dimension to the neglect of the emotional dimension is equally sinful. In other words, sin consists precisely in destroying the synthesis of the whole by emphasizing too intently one of the parts to the neglect of the others.

The Pharisee and the tax collector at prayer represent two of the many alternatives available to us in ordering and organizing our many experiences for meaning in our own lives.

Organizing Ourselves

First among the alternatives presented to us is that of buying into the American Dream, and directing our identities, our perspectives, and our ethics towards success. We would identify ourselves as primarily rational and individualistic, assume a perspective of autonomous independence, and pursue its ethics of wealth and status. Moreover, we would do so consistently and simultaneously, and relate to everyone and everything else on those terms.

Attuning ourselves to this course are several important implications. We are establishing relationships, but relationships grounded in autonomous independence. We relate to others on the basis of what they can do for us. Whatever else we might want to think or say, the fact of the matter is that we assess others on our terms, always asking the question: "What can you do for me?" We ask that of people, of nature, and of God. As long as they provide for us and satisfy our expectations, we value them. As long as they fulfill our needs, and do what we want, we keep them around. Otherwise, we discard them.

In our relationships with others, even our most intimate relationships, we are consumed with ourselves. We seek that perfect someone who will accommodate us, and contribute to the images we present to others. We say "I love you," but really mean "I love you because you love me." A serious career woman was once overheard to say, cynically and ironically, "I need a wife." What she really meant was that she wanted someone who would know her so well that her needs would be satisfied without having to verbalize them. She could, then, concentrate on what was important to her.

We might also say that we need God, something out there somewhere having ultimate power, especially the power to provide answers to our questions and satisfaction for our desires. We even view nature through these lenses, appreciating trees in general, or a tree in particular, for what it can do for us, whether supplying us with oxygen for our breathing, shade for our comfort, wood for our houses, or a pleasant scenario for our enjoyment.

Another implication is that this perspective on life does, in fact, enlist its own set of values. Those values are pursued primarily with respect to our own self-interests, to accompany our own objectives, to fulfill those objectives. Those are the values of the American Dream: wealth and status. Concentrating so intently on ourselves, we would appreciate other people, as well as nature, and even the divine as existing in opposition to us, to serve us, to satisfy us. That is, we would situate ourselves at the edge of the universe, and view the world through the lenses of selfishness and greed.

Another significant implication of this understanding of ourselves, our perspectives, and our ethics is that it exists. Whether from nature or nurture, there is something about us that is individual and autonomous, self-contained and independent. There is something about us that drives us and motivates us towards wealth and status, even towards selfishness and greed. To deny it, ignore it, or avoid it is unimaginable or inexcusable, perhaps even counterproductive.

A lot of good has arisen from people who have distinguished themselves and become wealthy by pursuing their own independence, even their own wealth. Detaching themselves from everyone and everything around them, using people and nature to create goods and services everyone wants and needs, they have contributed both to our lives in particular and to society in general. They have pulled into themselves, focused on their own self-interests, and harnessed their creativity and imagination to improve the quality of our lives.

Some have invented new or better products to make our lives easier, and to allow us time and energy to pursue the American Dream for ourselves. Some have provided insights and conclusions to help us understand and appreciate other people and nature. Some have even reflected the benefits of dedicating their lives to God.

The underlying question is one of motivation and objective. What is really going on here? Are they doing these things primarily for themselves, to boost their own egos, to achieve power and authority? Insofar as those are their driving motives, we can ascribe their identities, their perspectives, and their ethics to self-interest. These are questions we ask of men and women in business, especially of entrepreneurs and leaders in industry.

A second alternative is to direct our identities, our perspectives, and our ethics towards dependence, and towards surrender and compassion for others. We direct our time and energy towards caring and sacrifice for other people, whether immediately or remotely present to us. We want them to tell us what they want and what they need for satisfaction and fulfillment, and we do everything we can to meet their expectations. We ask: "What can I do for you?" We ask that question of everyone and everything existing outside of, and apart from, ourselves. We value them, cherish them, love them because we can sacrifice ourselves for them.

Moreover, that pursuit of dependence becomes the basis for assessing our relationships with others. Being "in relationship," to use a popular phrase, usually means setting someone apart, giving that someone priority in our lives, and attending to their needs and wants. We are consumed with providing for them, and love becomes a matter of surrender and compassion, of sacrifice and caring. They are first in our lives, and, more than anything, we want to please them.

People who dedicate their lives to others are often described as belonging to the "service professions" or "public service"— teachers, administrators, and support staffs of schools; doctors, nurses, aides, and administrators in hospitals; social workers and civil service employees, politicians and judges. They want to help others, to surrender and sacrifice themselves for others. They want to serve society and contribute to the common good.

We might even feel that way towards nature, and rather than using trees to meet our needs, direct our time and energy to meeting theirs by doing everything we can to preserve them and nurture them. The "tree huggers" of our world are dedicated to their care, and often at great sacrifice. We often see people making animals a priority in their lives, giving up opportunities for socializing or travelling to care for their pets.

Others search the scriptures or sacred writings of their respective religious traditions to discern the will of a personal God or transcendent principle. They want to commit themselves, dedicate themselves to "something other" than themselves or the world around them. This is the perspective of the influential nineteenth-century theologian Friedrich Schleiermacher who defines religion as "absolute dependence on God" and, in doing so, raises emotional dependence to ultimate significance.[2]

Dependence becomes more important than independence. So also do its values of surrender and compassion expressed in sacrifice and care. There is nothing we

---

[2] Patrick Primeaux, *Richard R. Niebuhr on Christ and Religion: The Four Stage Development of His Theology*, Toronto Studies in Theology (New York: Edwin Mellen, 1981), 73-87.

wouldn't do for another or others, for plants and animals, for God or some transcendent principle. Needless to say, there is something— even a great deal— to be said for people who make this pursuit of dependence a priority in their lives. They, too, contribute to the enrichment our lives and that of society.

The third alternative brings its focus to bear on interdependence as a priority motivating and directing our lives. These are people who move beyond the disconnections of independence and the connections of dependence into the interconnections of interdependence. For the most part, we identify them as religious, for they move into a realm transcending what we have become accustomed to describing as ordinary life.

They raise the bar, push the envelope to the edge, focusing on interrelationships and the possibilities of moving beyond relationships with ourselves, or others, or nature, or God in particular. They want to know how it all comes together, and adopt a perspective for their own lives, and life in general, which concentrates on all of them for a consistent and simultaneous appreciation of the whole. They tend towards abstraction and idealism, but, at the same time, towards translating that abstraction and idealism into implications for the everyday world of division and separation, tension and conflict.

These are the people the psychologist Abraham Maslow describes as having had "peak experiences."[3] They are the gurus, visionaries, and scholars of the world, appreciated and admired for keeping this dimension of experience in the forefront. Their focus is not on the particular, but on the general. They would connect even the identities, perspectives, and ethics we have defined with respect to dependence and independence, and move even beyond them for interdependence. That is, they would connect the "extrinsic utility" of independence to the "intrinsic quality" of dependence, and move even beyond those categories to appreciate all of life as

---

[3] Abraham Maslow, *Religions, Values, and Peak-Experiences* (London: Penguin Books, 1970).

interrelated and interconnected. They view the whole before its parts, the forest before the trees.

We mentioned that they are often described as religious because the divine is often depicted as establishing and maintaining all things in interconnected unity. However, the divine, as we have just seen, is also described with respect to independence and dependence. That is, it can be interpreted as meeting the expectations of self-interest or others-interest. In either case, however, each of those interpretations is consistent with the manner in which we relate to ourselves, to others, and to nature from either point of view.

Other alternatives are also available to us. Rather than choosing one and disregarding the others, we can emphasize one, relegate another to secondary consideration, and ignore the third. The American Dream does that when it imposes autonomous independence as so dominant that it barely leaves room for communal dependence, and totally ignores interdependence. There is also the possibility we have been proposing: to join all three perspectives into a single integrated synthesis of the whole.

Basic to an appreciation of this synthesis is an acknowledgment of knowledge as unified before divided, and of experience as reflective of that unity and synthesis. From experience we know ourselves to be independent, dependent, and interdependent. We know from experience that there is something about us that would disconnect us from one another, connect us to one another, and interconnect us to the totality of experienced reality.

We also know that to direct our attention to one or the other necessarily results in gains and losses. To concentrate on one to the neglect of the others, we lose the opportunities afforded by the others. Within the American Dream, to dedicate ourselves entirely to the pursuit of success implies certain gains, especially with respect to wealth and distinction. However, it means that we lose the opportunities to pursue either happiness or bliss. To avail ourselves to the opportunities afforded by all three, we would have to establish a synthesis of all three.

To do that in America, we would have to reinvent the American Dream for ourselves. We would have to reinvent the American Dream for the other people and for the institutions that influence us, and make demands on us, and who we, in turn, influence and make demands on. We cannot reinvent either ourselves or the American Dream alone, or in isolation from others or the institutions to which we belong.

Organizing Business

That process of reorganization and reinvention is already taking place within the institutions of the American experience. It is marked by a subtle change in direction from dictating to following, from commanding to serving, from demanding to listening. On the political scene, for example, politicians are paying serious attention to the moods and preferences of their constituents in formulating policy, setting priorities, and projecting an image appealing to voters. Religion, too, has become more attentive to meeting the needs of people rather than imposing expectations on them. Even in schools, teachers are more attentive to facilitating learning rather than lecturing. In our families, changes are taking place which challenge the traditional role of the father as the exclusive head of the household and attribute greater authority to the mother.

If Norman Lear is right, and business has superceded the roles of all of these institutions for setting ethical standards of conduct and behavior, we can expect changes in business, too. From a management perspective, there has been a recognizable change in the locus of decision-making authority. Rarely is it the prerogative of senior management to dictate policies and procedures without consulting others. The degree to which others are included within the decision-making process has, in fact, become the basic criterion for identifying the company's culture and values.

Is the company managed primarily for production, primarily for people, or for both? Underlying each of these management objectives are personal ones. Is the company managed primarily for independence, or dependence, or both? In other words, in its organizational structure every company reflects an underlying appreciation of the person as driven towards self-interest or others-interest. Emphasis on the first designates a company's culture and structure as authoritative; on the second as participative; on the third as affiliative.

The authoritative organization is so familiar to us it hardly warrants description. It refers to the typical hierarchical structure in which we study, work, and worship. Hierarchy immediately calls to minds a series of ranks and levels arranged in descending order of authority and obedience with few at the top and many at the bottom. It is often depicted as a pyramid with a pointed top and a flat bottom. Because decision-making is relegated to the few senior managers at the pyramid's apex, and its authority imposed onto the rank and file, we call it an authoritative organization.

This managerial structure corresponds to the perspective focused on independence, especially in its emphasis on the person as an autonomous individual. It is also rational in its emphasis on production. It clearly charts progression from the beginning to the end of the production process, and also just as clearly defines the role of each person within that process.

What is not as clear is that the structure of the hierarchical organization demands adherence to a certain set of values to maintain and sustain its objectives. The business ethicist John Haughey, S.J. lists these values as competition, profitability, productivity, and efficiency.[4] Moreover, he describes them as grounded in, and arising from an "economic rationality" which, in theory and practice, assumes a "willingness to sacrifice or instrumentalize people" to meet the company's objectives.

The authoritatively structured company does not only use people. It also uses nature, and directs both people and nature towards its objectives. To do that, it enlists a set of values. For Haughey, competition implies an orientation towards success, and demands rugged aggression and individualism for its attainment. Profitability is directed towards financial security, which, in turn, requires selfishness and greed. Productivity and efficiency focus on tasks rather than people so that relationships become remote and unimportant.

All of these words point to one thing: a perspective of autonomous independence, an identity grounded in rational propositions, an ethical code directed to the pursuit of wealth and distinction. The company adopts that perspective, identity, and ethical code for its corporate culture, vision, and mission. It also adopts it for its managers and employees, demanding that they adopt it for themselves.

To maintain this structure and objectives, the company has to impose obedience as its primary virtue. Because of that, the company also has to impose rules and regulations, elaborate and detailed policies and procedures. It also has to police

---

[4] John Haughey, "As I See It," *Company*, Winter, 1987, 30.

them, and, to do that offers rewards and punishments as incentives.

Are these managers and employees happy? Who cares? It's not a matter of happiness. It's a matter of success. In fact, they are not happy. The managerial guru Rensis Likert points out that, because of the inherent division of people into leaders and followers, employees assume attitudes of subservience "toward superiors coupled with hostility," and managers assume attitudes of "contempt for subordinates."[5] That is not surprising because, as we're all aware, a higher status implies greater wealth and distinction. Those who have made it look down on those who haven't. Those who haven't made it want to, and resent those who have.

Because of its overwhelming emphasis on success reflected in production and profit, the authoritative company values people and nature only insofar as they contribute to production and profit. However, in the early twentieth century, a reaction to this valuation of people gradually came to the fore as companies began to realize that attending to people, and to their needs, resulted in higher production quotas and profit ratios.

Now companies are managing for people as well as profits. That change in management objective has precipitated a change in company structure and corporate culture. It has also precipitated a change in company values. The authoritative organization has given way to the participative organization.

The participative organization retains the basic structure of the hierarchical organization, but moves it into the background. As the structure recedes, so does the company's absorption with production and profit as its only objective. So also does the value system needed to support and maintain both organizational structure and strategic objective. What moves to the fore is attention to people, but less as objects valued for their utility, and more as subjects valued for their intrinsic dignity.

---

[5] Rensis Likert, *New Patterns of Management* (New York: McGraw-Hill, 1961), 225.

That dignity is often defined with respect to participation in decision-making. The company, then, surrenders something of itself, something of its decision-making authority, and diffuses it among employees. Employees are, in turn, encouraged to adopt the values of surrender and compassion among one another. That encouragement is translated into structure as people are gathered into small groups to make decisions for their own particular areas of concern. They participate in decision-making, and also in the exercise of authority.

The participative organization is usually depicted as circular, with each area of concern represented by a circle connected to other circles to comprise the whole. As people relate to one another, cooperation becomes the dominant virtue, and surrender and compassion translate into caring and sacrificing for one another, i.e., for the objectives of the group. As corporate structure changes, so do corporate virtues and values.

With cooperation replacing obedience as the dominant ethical virtue, policies and procedures are loosened. Rewards and punishments are less emphasized, and resentment and hostility between followers and leaders recede into the background. If not happy, people are happier in the participative organization than in the hierarchical organization.

The participative organization, then, places a premium on happiness. It also places a premium on the kinds of relationships that lend themselves to happiness. That is because they value dependence more than independence. It is also because they manage people as well as production.

There is also a growing concern for the environment accompanying this concern for people. That, too, is consistent with dependence, and with its emphasis on the intrinsic dignity of nature. Some companies are even identifying their corporate cultures and ethical codes with respect to the environment.

Perhaps the clearest testimony to this recognition of independence and dependence within a company is Tom Chappell's *The Soul of a Business*. Chappell is Chairman and CEO of Tom's of Maine, which produces natural tooth pastes and cleaning supplies. He has created the company with his wife, Kate, from a deep-seated "respect for humanity and nature."[6]

As his business grew, he brought in "young MBAs and alumni of big packaged goods companies," who, in pursuit of profit, wanted to add artificial flavoring to the natural toothpaste. Influenced by them and by their professional expertise, he relinquished his creative, entrepreneurial spirit and focused on "new account development, new advertising campaigns, financial planning, financial control, management reorganization and evaluations, and new equipment."[7] Becoming frustrated with himself and the direction the business was going, he lost interest.

He decided on a mid-life change of career. He would become an Episcopalian minister. However, following consultation with others, he decided to study theology to learn what he could of ministry, but to apply what he had learned to his business. He entered Harvard Divinity School, and was inspired by several of his teachers.

From the moral philosopher Arthur Dyck, Chappell learned the distinction between "utility" and "formalism." Utility implied "running a business by the numbers," and formalism referred to "that inner sense of obligation and human connection that people feel for their friends, neighbors, and family."[8] From Richard R. Niebuhr, Chappell learned of the Jewish philosopher, Martin Buber, and his distinction between "I-Thou" and "I-It" relationships which he interpreted as that between "people versus things" and "the dignity of persons versus their utility." Chappell, however, also learned that "Buber believed that both relations ought to be

---

[6] Tom Chappell, *The Soul of A Business: Managing for profit and the Common Good* (New York: Bantam Books, 1993), xiii.

[7] Tom Chappell, 5.

[8] Tom Chappell, 11.

integrated into our lives, that to be fully human we can approach the world from the mind and from the spirit. We can respect what we also use."[9]

What Chappell did not learn was the interdependence of the spiritual, for an appreciation of infinity and transcendence would not allow for anyone or anything to be used. It would defy any attempt to use the words respect and use in the same context. That realization is, in itself, proof that Chappell does not understand the spiritual, or the implications of transcendence and infinity for himself, for his relationships with others, or for his business.

What Chappell really learned at Harvard were the underlying values of the participative organization, for he would return home to dismantle the authoritative structure of Tom's of Maine, and replace it with a participative structure. He would be attentive to people and to nature, but continue to use them as objects valued for their usefulness to the business. To be sure, he would respect them, but for their utility and for their dignity: "I eventually agreed that people have to be *useful* in producing products, sales, and profits, but they also have to be respected, and that includes sharing in the company's success."[10]

He not only reorganized the business for participation in decision-making, but also instituted programs like profit sharing to express his new appreciation for the company's employees and their contribution to profit. He also focused his attention on building community among employees, and between the employees and the customers, and the employees and the community in which Tom's of Maine was located. His emphasis on forging connections reflected a basic change in paradigm with an equal emphasis on the structure and objectives of independence and dependence.

Not only would the company's structure and objectives change, so would its

---

[9] Tom Chappell, 13.
[10] Tom Chappell, 11.

identity, perspective, and values. Tom's of Maine would give as well as take, surrendering to others and benefiting from others. The values of surrender and compassion would move to the foreground as those of wealth and distinction moved into the background.

Chappell learned that he had lost the opportunities afforded by a perspective of dependence. He realized that he had lost interest in the company precisely because he had placed too much emphasis on the opportunities afforded by independence. Unfortunately, he did not learn what he had to lose by ignoring the opportunities of interdependence.

The use of the word "soul" in the title of his book, as well as his appeal to perspectives and values learned at Harvard Divinity School, signal a spiritual dimension directing the transition from the hierarchical to the participative organization. However, there is nothing spiritual about it at all. His book would be better titled "The Heart of a Business." Like so many others, Chappell has confused the emotional with the spiritual, and subsumed the spiritual into the emotional.

That absorption of the spiritual into the emotional is accompanied by the absorption of interdependence into dependence. It is also accompanied by a loss of attention to mystery and transcendence. Pleased with his own transition from a focus on self-interest and success to a focus on others-interest and happiness, he has stopped short of the opportunities afforded by a focus on the interconnections and interrelationships experienced in bliss.

There are two problems with the participative organization. It can easily move in two different directions. It can concentrate so much on dependence, and on managing people, that it can lose sight of independence. That is, it can focus so intently on happiness that it can lose sight of success, and also of the need to maintain and sustain the organization through profit maximization. On, the other maintain and sustain the organization through profit maximization. On, the other hand, it can easily continue to use people to meet its own objectives and to lead them into identifying happiness with success. For the management consultant William Roth this would represent a subtle form of manipulation where "instead of being programmed simply to produce more, they are now being programmed to enjoy producing more."[11]

In response to either of those two possibilities, management theorists are recommending a fusion or affiliation of the two, with equal weight given to the demands of success and those of happiness. They are encouraging an integration of perspectives which would focus attention on both the rational and emotional determinants of corporate identity, the independence and the dependence of organizational perspective, and the values of both for a comprehensive company ethic.

The affiliative organization would not seek some kind of parallel accommodation of the two, but rather an integrative fusion of the two into a single corporate identity, perspective, and ethical code. It would be directed towards a synthesis where the two converge into one unified point of view for both motivation and objective. The virtues of surrender and compassion would be evident within the pursuit of wealth and distinction, and vice versa. This would mean that the two sets of values would enter into any decision-making process.

The former Secretary of the Treasury Robert Reich suggests that this affiliative organization is not simply a figment of someone's imagination, but an already existing reality. He describes, for example, Trilogy Software, Inc., "a small, rapidly growing software firm based in Austin, Texas," where "to call Trilogy workers 'employees' misses the point. They're all shareholders. They're all managers. They're all partners."[12]

---

[11] William Roth, *The Evolution of Management Theory* (Orefield, PA: Roth and Associates, 1993), 38.
[12] Robert Reich, The Company of the Future," *Fast Company*, November, 1998, 127.

For Reich this translates into corporate "glue." Corporate glue cannot be confined to the values of others-interest. It assumes them as already-existing. It also assumes the values of wealth and distinction. When people come to work, they want to move beyond the determinants of both self-interest and others-interest. For the Xerox Parc guru John Seely Brown the search for success and happiness has been assumed into a search for meaning in both the private and the public sphere. "Talented people," he claims, "want to be part of something they can believe in, something that confers meaning on their work and on their lives."[13] In the name of meaning, all of the distinctions between dependence and independence, work and life, outside and inside lose significance.

Corporate glue is identified with respect to meaning, and meaning to doing something that "makes a difference," "advances a larger purpose," offers people "something they can believe in," and "spiritual goals that energize an organization by resonating with the personal values of people who work there."[14] This meaning they find not only at Xerox and Trilogy, but at Isaacson, Miller, "a Boston-based boutique head-hunting firm," Lovelace Institutes, "a biomedical-research institute based in Albuquerque," Ernst & Young LLP's Center for Business Innovation in Cambridge, Massachusetts.

> *These companies offer many of the advantages of free agency: flexibility in how, when, and where you work; compensation linked to what you contribute; freedom to move from project to project. But they also offer the advantages of belonging to an organization in which mutual commitment builds continuity.[15]*

Is the organization changing people's perspectives and values? Are people's perspectives and values changing the organization? Both seem to be happening at the same time. As organizations are changing so are people. David Bellshaw, working for a Boston-based boutique head-hunting firm, tells us that "we are vicariously

---

[13] Robert Reich, 132.
[14] Robert Reich, 132.
[15] Robert Reich, 127.

saving the world through our clients."[16]   Chris Meyer, of Ernst & Young LLP's Center for Business Innovation in Cambridge, Massachusetts, explains that "... people are attracted to the company because working here helps them become better than they would be otherwise" and how

> ... *coming here, you're learning not just how to identify the issues of the future but also how to do the work of the future... Working in the knowledge economy requires the ability to recognize patterns, to share ideas with people inside and outside your organization, to maintain relationships with people who have common interests, and pull value out of those relationships.*[17]

Those relationships, however, are not those of the participative organization's emphasis on team cooperation or surrender. They are ascribed to a broader context, with an eye towards the future, moving beyond restrictions of the present towards the possibility of the infinite. Moreover, they do so with a passion Reich compares to "missionary zeal."[18]

On the level of virtue, obedience and cooperation are integrated into commitment as, with respect to perspective, independence and dependence have converged into something which is, at this point illusive and indefinable, but which seems to be pointing towards interdependence. It's not quite there yet, but seems to be moving towards a sensibility to mystery and transcendence.

The affiliative organization does not yet include interdependence, at least to the extent we might expect. The interest in making a difference, serving a larger purpose, and pursuing something to believe in is still confined to the immediacy of the world, and to experiences within the present. There is no mention, even

---

[16] Robert Reich, 134.

[17] Robert Reich, 140.

[18] Robert Reich, 134. "Bellshaw comes to this calling naturally: His father was a Baptist minister, and so was his grandfather. 'I rebelled against my background, and I still do— very actively' Bellshaw says. "But in some funny way, given my genes and upbringing, my work is a secular way of doing what my family has done. Two generations of ministers, and I broke the mold. Yet there remains a mission-driven theme in my life."

implicitly, of spirituality with respect to the transcendence and infinity which surpasses the boundaries and limitations of time and place.

Chappell, for example, is proud of his company's outward perspective reflected in its concern for the immediate community in which it exists, and for contributing to environmental preservation. He is also proud of the realization that these concerns reflect spiritual values. In some remote way, they do. But, they are values limited to the immediate rather than to the infinite, to time and place rather than to transcendence.

Recapping and Moving Ahead

Referring to his religious music, the jazz composer Duke Ellington "insisted on a difference between talking to God and, as he described his own efforts, 'people talking to people about God.'"[19] Ellington is expressing a real difference between relating to people and relating to the divine, and also acknowledging a tendency to identify one with the other. When referring to the values of dependence, all we have to do is mention God, and somehow surrender and compassion become sacred.

That is true also of independence. Any new insight or discovery arising from prayer is immediately attributed to the divine, even when the motivation and objective of prayer is enhanced self-interest. The spiritual, however, is different from the rational and from the emotional. Its perspective and its values cannot be reduced to either independence or dependence.

These tendencies towards reduction of the spiritual are not confined to individuals. They also arise in discussions of business mission and vision, structure and values. When men and women in business talk to other men and women in business about God, it does not mean that they are referring to interdependence, or to mystery and transcendence. Rather, it usually means that they are referring to a new awareness of something about themselves, or of something about other people and nature.

Writing for the *Washington Post*, Don Oldenburg explains how "terms such as 'holistic' and 'commitment' are finding their way into corporate vernacular—describing workers who are fully engaged in their work and bring passion and energy to it and work environments that nourish it."[20] As we read on we realize just how much these words refer to independence and dependence.

Judi Neal, a management professor, is quoted: "'There are thousands of people for whom spirituality is very important... It's important to them to be of service to others, to see the divinity in others, to make a heart connection with people, and to be forgiving.'" Whatever she means by the word "divine" it is clear from the context that she is referring to something human rather than to "something other" than ourselves, other persons, and nature.

Clearly, she has collapsed the divine into the human, the values of interdependence into those of dependence. Jones, however, does claim that "'something has been stirring in people's souls— a longing for deeper meaning, deeper connection, greater simplicity, a connection to something higher.'" Deeper, higher, greater than what? The antecedents to her claims are the values of the independently-structured workplace which, in the words of Laurie Beth Jones, reflect "undervaluing people, assigning them herculean tasks without giving them the

---

[19] Ben Ratliff, "Just the Best in Ellington's Sacred Works," *New York Times*, December 11, 1999, B11.
[20] Don Oldenburg, "Spirituality at Work: Linking Joy, Meaning, Commitment & the Company's Bottom Line," *Washington Post*, April 15, 1999.

authority to carry out the tasks… the verbal and mental abuse."[21]

The reaction to the extremes and abuses of the pursuit of wealth and distinction is giving rise to a "more human" workplace where the surrender and compassion of dependence are being implemented. Michael Jones, an organizational behavior expert, describes the need for spirituality as "a new intelligence of the heart," appealing to "a deeper compassion for one another." These are, for Oldenburg, "spiritual principles."

There is yet no mention of spirituality in business, or of an appeal to the divine, or mention of God with respect to mystery and transcendence. Why? In his original definition of the American Dream, Adams is so focused on economic wealth and distinction, that he ignores both the human and the divine. Neither the values of dependence nor independence would interfere with the new economic "social order" he is recommending for the future.

When two generations later, Kasser and Ryan added the virtues of dependence to those of independence in their definition of the American Dream they were reflecting a growing consciousness, a progression in perspective. They were demonstrating that the new social order envisioned by Adams would focus not only on self-interest, but also on others-interest.

That same development is occurring within institutionalized religion. Within the same seventy years between Adams and Kasser and Ryan, religion has moved from a preoccupation with God for the individual to God for the many. It has shifted focus from a relationship with God for oneself and one's self-interest to a relationship with God reflected in relationships with other people, and even to preserving the environment.[22]

---

[21] Don Oldenburg. Jones is the writer of two books, *Jesus CEO* (Hyperion) and *The Path: Creating Your Mission Statement for Work and Life* (Hyperion).
[22] David Gonzalez, "Religions are Putting Faith in Environmentalism," *New York Times*, November 6, 1994.

It has also led to a shift in values. No longer focused on individual sins, religion has focused on social sins and systemic sins. Its emphasis is on sin as a fracture or breach in relationships with others. That same emphasis questions the causes or origins of those chasms and fractures, and grounds them in the systems and institutions of the social order organized to divide and isolate people from one another.

The contemporary theologian Paul Surlis grounds even the emphasis on individualized sin in institutional systems. He claims 'the teaching that the act of intercourse must always be open to procreation" is based neither in Jewish theology nor the teaching of Jesus, but on "Stoicism with its emphasis on nature and biological function, and its rejection of pleasure and erotic love as valid purposes for sexuality in marriage."[23] This observation leads to a question: "This raises the question of whether or not sexual teaching is being instrumentalized to serve political purposes related to institutional maintenance or control...?"[24]

Rather, Christian morality should be directed to others-interest. "It is clear from the Gospels that the thrust of Jesus's message, ministry, table-fellowship, and prayer," writes Surlis, "was the inauguration of the rule, reign, or kingdom of God."[25] This means that the church would interpret the Gospels and Christian ethics from an emotional perspective, and concentrate on others-interest:

> *The poor, disease-ridden, oppressed, and marginalized, especially children, slaves, and women, were the focus of his efforts. Jesus was concerned with abuses of religion, of power and prestige which allowed affluence and privileged status to some while consigning others to poverty, hunger, disease, and loss of human dignity and status at the bottom of the human pyramid.*[26]

That shift in emphasis from self-interest to others-interest has resulted in what

---

[23] Paul Surlis, "Moral Theology: A Tradition to be Rejected? Toward a New Paradigm in Moral Argument," in *The Church in the Nineties, Its legacy, Its Future,* ed., Pierre M. Hegy (Collegeville, MN: Liturgical Press, 1993), 43.
[24] Paul Surlis, 44.
[25] Paul Surlis, 44.

theologian Edward Vacek, S.J. has described as an equation of the divine with the human. He claims that the first great commandment (love of God) has been collapsed into the second (love of neighbor):

When I ask my students, "What do you mean by love for God?" they usually give one of four answers. Some volunteer that loving God means keeping the commandments, like not killing or stealing. Most say that loving God means helping one's neighbor. The more theologically educated add that it means taking care of the poor. Lastly, those steeped in our psychological age share that loving God means caring for one's own deepest self.[27]

With the exception of the fourth, all of the answers pertain to the others-interest of dependence, to surrender and compassion. The last, of course, focuses on independence and self-interest. Vacek notes that "atheists affirm these four practices."[28] If that is the case, there is no need of God for grounding either self-interest or others-interest.

Moral theology has not always taught the values of dependence as primary. The overpowering influence of rational independence, and its values wealth and distinction have been absorbed into moral theology. Writing at the mid-point of the twentieth century, Henry Davis claimed that "employees are bound to provide their employers reasonable honor and respect, service and obedience."[29]

He also claimed that "the master is bound to treat the worker in a humane way," but only "as far as the nature of the work permits."[30] The employer, i.e., "the master," is also encouraged to pay a just wage, "that amount of wage which will keep him and his wife and family in frugal comfort, commensurate with the conditions of life of the normal worker of his class."[31] The moral obligations of the employer are, clearly, minimal, especially when contrasted with those of the worker:

---

[26] Paul Surlis, 44.
[27] Edward Collins Vacek, "The Eclipse of Love for God," *America*, 174:8, March 9, 1996, 13-14.
[28] Edward Collins Vacek, 14.
[29] Henry Davis, *Moral and Pastoral Theology, Volume II* (London: Sheed & Ward, 1959), 80.
[30] Henry Davis, 80.

They sin by arousing against their master unfounded discontent. It is certain that they violate strict justice— as well as charity— if they neglect their duties, if they do not give a fair day's work for a fair day's wage, if they unreasonably diminish output whilst taking a good wage, since this is a species of covert hostility... [32]

With respect to the obligations of the employer, the word sin is not used, although "serious obligation" and "scandal" are mentioned, but within a context which suggests less gravity and severity.[33]

What this theological perspective reflects is not only acceptance and approval of the authoritative organization, but a rational demonstration of rights and duties based on the quantitative distinctions inherent to that organizational structure. In effect, Davis is proposing moral directives which assume the hierarchical organization, and which are consistent with its structure. He does not question the organization itself. Nor does he assess the values inherent to the organization, and its appropriation by managers and workers for other areas of their lives.

Moral theology assumes two different perspectives, as we do for our lives. This second perspective is continuous with the American Dream's focus on self-interest. The first might, then, be attributed to resistance to the abuses and exaggerations of the first. What is important, though, is that underlying each of these alternative perspectives is an accompanying appreciation of God. God would want us to focus first on our own self-interest. God would want us to focus first on others-interest.

It is this distinction, and the exaggerated emphasis on one or the other that leads Karen Armstrong, the British historian and moralist, to suggest that "we may need a time without God."[34] The implication is that images of God originating in either independence or dependence are no longer valid or meaningful.

---

[31] Henry Davis, 81.
[32] Henry Davis, 82.
[33] Henry Davis, 80-84.
[34] Karen Armstrong, "We May Need a Time Without God," *New York Newsday*, February 6, 1995.

The atheism we have in parts of Europe is no bad thing because atheism has often been a transitional mode of faith. We may have to walk away from old, outworn ideas of God that no longer work. Some of our human images of God are not absolute and may need to be knocked down. A passionate, committed atheism can be more religious than a weary, tired theism, a conventional, unthinking theism, especially if the theism does not express itself in compassion. We may need a period, at least in Europe, of being without God for awhile— a silence, an apartness in a cloud of unknowing— so something creative can happen in the future.[35]

How will our images of God change? Perhaps the old images of God created in the likeness of either independence or dependence need to be questioned. Perhaps they need to be rejected, especially when exaggerated. Perhaps a new one will arise from recognition and awareness of these exaggerations.

That expectation is not unreasonable. We have already experienced a shift of emphasis from a focus on self-interest to a focus on others-interest. We have also seen it has resulted in a greater appreciation of dependence for our self-knowledge and self-worth. We now identify ourselves, our perspectives, and our values with respect to independence and dependence. Even, then, we are pursuing the American Dream, especially as it coincides with a major shift in paradigm reflected in the organizations of business.

Can we begin to broaden that paradigm to include direct reference to interdependence in both theory and practice, mission statement and mission implementation, organizational structure and corporate culture? Can the mystery and transcendence we often attribute to God be mentioned within the same sentence as business? Can it be mentioned within the same sentence as life itself?

We can, but only if we want to have meaningful lives. We already have meaningful lives. Influenced by the American Dream, we have attributed meaning to wealth and distinction first, and compassion and surrender second. Yet, the progression of business organizations from concentration on the first, to

---

[35] Karen Arstrong, *New York Newsday*.

concentration on the second, then to concentration on both, is paving the way for an additional perspective.

That does not mean, however, that we dismiss independence and dependence to concentrate on interdependence. Rather, it means that we concentrate on all three simultaneously and consistently, maintaining and sustaining them within the delicate and fragile equilibrium of integrated synthesis.

As we are not composed of mind, heart, or soul, neither are our perspectives of independence, dependence, or interdependence exclusive of one another. Neither are our values of wealth and distinction, surrender and compassion, transcendence and mystery. Neither are the virtues of obedience, cooperation, and commitment.

As the organizations of business are being reinvented, as we as persons are being reinvented, so, too, is the American Dream. It is being reinvented to incorporate the virtue of commitment and the values of transcendence and infinity into the already existing virtues and values of independence and dependence.

What will it look like? What form will it assume, especially at that point where abstraction meets practice, where the rubber meets the road? No one really knows, at least not at this point in its development. Yet, all indications point to its realization.

The question is whether we will be ready for it. The implications of the use of the internet within business and of the globalization of business are indicators that there is a thrust forward, even towards the infinite. They are indicating even a predisposition towards transcendence by eliminating the limitations imposed by self-interest and others-interest. They are pointing to the interests of the whole, of the totality of experience, and to a convergence of disconnections, connections, and inter-connections— of success, happiness, and bliss.

As this process is taking place, we find ourselves in transition. We question ourselves, our identities, our perspectives, and our ethics. We question the influences we have received from the outside, and also their expectations of us. We do so with respect to ourselves as persons, and with respect to the organizations which give form and shape to our lives.

In both, we seek meaning, and realize that meaning will not proceed from any kind of either/or myopic mission or vision. Even more significantly, what we realize is that we want to create meaning for ourselves as persons, and for our organizations as corporate persons. As Robert Reich demonstrated in his description of the affiliative organization, meaning is attributed to a convergence of concern for oneself, for others and nature, and for that "something other" than either of these. Meaning is not, then, a matter of emphasizing one or the other, but of a synthesis of all three for a new appreciation of what it means to be a person living and working in America.

Sources For
Chapter 6: Reinterpreting

For the Parable of the Pharisee and the Tax Collector

Henry Wansbrough, ed., "The Gospel of Luke," 18:9-13, *The New Jerusalem Bible* (Garden City, NY: Doubleday & Company, 1985).

For the Distinction Between the Emotional and the Spiritual

Patrick Primeaux, *Richard R. Niebuhr on Christ and Religion: The Four Stage Development of His Theology*, Toronto Studies in Theology (New York: Edwin Mellen, 1981).

Abraham Maslow, *Religions, Values, and Peak-Experiences* (London: Penguin Books, 1970).

For the Values of the Authoritative Organization

John Haughey, "As I See It," *Company*, Winter, 1987.

Rensis Likert, *New Patterns of Management* (New York: McGraw-Hill, 1961).

For the Values of the Participative Organization

Tom Chappell, *The Soul of A Business: Managing for profit and the Common Good* (New York: Bantam Books, 1993).

William Roth, *The Evolution of Management Theory* (Orefield, PA: Roth and Associates, 1993).

For the Values of the Affiliative Organization

Robert Reich, The Company of the Future," *Fast Company*, November, 1998.
For the Reduction of Interdependence to Dependence and Independence

Ben Ratliff, "Just the Best in Ellington's Sacred Works," *New York Times*, December 11, 1999.

Don Oldenburg, "Spirituality at Work: Linking Joy, Meaning, Commitment & the Company's Bottom Line," *Washington Post*, April 15, 1999.

David Gonzalez, "Religions are Putting Faith in Environmentalism," *New York Times*, November 6, 1994.

Paul Surlis, "Moral Theology: A Tradition to be Rejected? Toward a New Paradigm in Moral Argument," in *The Church in the Nineties, Its legacy, Its Future*, ed., Pierre M. Hegy (Collegeville, MN: Liturgical Press, 1993).

Edward Collins Vacek, "The Eclipse of Love for God," *America*, 174:8, March 9, 1996.

Henry Davis, *Moral and Pastoral Theology, Volume II* (London: Sheed & Ward, 1959).

Karen Armstrong, "We May Need a Time Without God," *New York Newsday*, February 6, 1995.

Index